JULIUS CAESAR · THE GALLIC WARS

JULIUS CAESAR

THE GALLIC WARS

---

*A translation by John Warrington with a preface by
John Mason Brown & an introduction by the translator.
Illustrated with engravings by
Bruno Bramanti*

COLLECTOR'S EDITION

Bound in Genuine Leather

The Easton Press

NORWALK, CONNECTICUT

CONTENTS

PREFACE

PREFACE

There was fire in the older man's eyes as he handed the book to the tall youth. 'This was written yesterday,' he said. 'It will be your exciting privilege to discover a new writer.' The older man was Professor George Martin Lane, apparently the only one of the many Greek and Latin scholars on the Harvard faculty in 1859 who taught the classics not as drier-than-dust exercises in grammar and memory but as volumes very much alive. The book was 'The Republic', and the undergraduate Oliver Wendell Holmes, son of the author of 'The Autocrat'.

Catherine Drinker Bowen tells this story in her warm and brilliant biography of Holmes. The story does not stop there. After Holmes had devoted his six weeks' winter vacation to reading 'The Republic' he wrote a fifteen-page paper about it in which Plato came off badly. At least young Holmes thought he did, and was so pleased with the result that he decided to submit his essay to the University Quarterly. Before doing so, however, he concluded it would be sensible and gratifying to show it to someone not professionally connected with Harvard.

His choice of a reader would have frightened you and me. It did not frighten young Holmes. He turned to his father's friend, Emerson, as a matter of course, and gave him his paper the next time he dropped by the doctor's house. Emerson sat down in the big leather chair by the fire and read it while its author fidgeted on the sofa. Upon finishing it Emerson arranged the sheets neatly, held them out to Wendell, and shook his head. 'When you shoot at a king you must kill him.'

That was all Emerson said. It was enough to cause young Holmes to take his fifteen pages upstairs and fling them in the *wastebasket. A month later Emerson came by again. 'Have you given Plato another chance?' he asked, smiling kindly. 'Hold Plato at arm's length as you have been doing, Wendell. That's good. But say to yourself, "Plato – you have pleased the world for two thousand years. Now let's see if you can please me."'*

I lean heavily on Mrs. Bowen's story of Holmes's introduction to Plato because I find it as wise as it is winning. The words of both Harvard's Professor Lane and Emerson seem to me to be words that ought to be remembered – and borrowed – by all those faced with the challenging task of teaching the classics. They are words which also have much to say to general readers who limit their adult reading to the latest books and avoid the standbys from antiquity (even in translation) as if they were bound to be dead and deadly merely because they are the products of the past. Surely critics, foolhardy enough to try to annihilate a work that has survived the centuries, would do well, before taking aim, to remember Emerson's 'When you shoot at a king you must kill him.'

The attitude toward the classics of most people supposedly educated, or at least exposed at great expense to what is identified as education in this country, is odd, to put it mildly. I write as no classicist, indeed as one who, having less than little Latin and no Greek, can read the writings of Greece and Rome only in translation.

But this I do know. Wander into the lounge car of a train carrying an English version of 'The Republic', or Horace's Odes, or Plutarch's Lives, and the man sitting next to you will either avoid conversation or, if he does decide to talk, address you as 'Professor' or 'Doc'. Speak of reading Thucydides or Xenophon to a chance companion at a dinner party, and that person is apt to think you are putting on airs and pretending to be a doubledome.

Why we should be afraid of the proven best; why we should be at ease only with the topical, the mediocre, or the inferior; why, spending millions as we do on education, it should be fashionable to forget it once we have finished college; and why we should be ready to doubt as pretenders or ridicule as oddities persons whose curiosity does not stop with their own times and who, without being highbrows, find real pleasure in turning back to classics are among the greatest and most depressing of American mysteries.

Perhaps it is because many who do the teaching fail to see the present in the past or the past in the present. Perhaps it is because in the realm of books they draw the same foolish and pleasure-denying distinction between the antique and the modern that those luckless mortals do, young or old, who are always age-conscious in their choice of friends and hence cheat themselves of countless delights by failing to realize that all persons are contemporaries if only their interests overlap.

Perhaps it is because teachers too often teach from the book alone, bringing no more experience to the text than their students do, and therefore making their instruction as dull and juiceless as only book knowledge can be when it is unrelated to any knowledge of life.

Never having studied the techniques of teaching as taught in Education courses up and down this land, I realize the risks I run in seeming to offer suggestions to teachers who, against their will, are often as overinstructed in the how's of teaching as they are underinstructed in the subjects they are supposed to teach. The last thing I mean to do is to poach on lands dear to and thoroughly explored by specialists. I do not know Latin or Greek. I do not teach them and have no desire to do so. I have in mind only adult readers who are reading for pleasure and can turn to translations without being penalized for depending on 'trots'. I trust, therefore, I may be forgiven if I confine myself to one classic and relate, for the little it may be worth, the surprising because agreeable experience I have recently had in rereading it or, as Emerson would say, in giving it another chance.

Had anyone suggested to me when I was a boy in school that 'The Gallic Wars' by one Julius Caesar would ever please me, or that I would read it as if it had been written yesterday by an author I was happy to discover, I would have laughed long and impolitely in that person's face. That is, of course, if I had not struggled to muster the kindness due a madman.

I would not have been alone in my laughter. An army of boys and girls, coerced into facing Caesar in classrooms everywhere, would have joined me. Few books, I'll wager, have been read by the young with greater disrelish than 'De Bello Gallico', few have been found duller, and few hated over the centuries with a more mutinous violence.

The conspirators who killed Caesar for me in my youth were many. Whether they are as numerous in a world in which the young have been brought up on war, are accustomed to scanning communiqués, seeing battle maps in each day's newspapers, and having their fathers or older brothers in uniform, I cannot say. Yet I suspect they are. First among these assassins count the fact that to most youngsters in school Caesar is not a man or an author but an assignment. His legions are not armies; they are lessons. No matter how many battles they win, they are to a certain extent defeated before they start. So is Caesar at his most victorious. The curse of the classroom is upon them one and all.

But the classroom, though inescapably a place where pleasure is imperiled by being coupled with obligation, does not have to be a curse and frequently is not. It depends upon the teacher no

*less than upon what is being taught. Caesar and his world might
have lived for me and my fellow sufferers in our youth (as both
of them managed to survive in Shakespeare's tragedy – another
assignment) if only we had known enough Latin to read him
with ease and had not tackled him as if he were a dictionary.
He might, too, have enjoyed a better chance if, instead of being
taught by a person as peaceful as a dove, he had been introduced
by someone who knew something about war.*

*Those endless marches, those countless camps, those bellicose
tribes, and that bridge (oh, that bridge!) – for years the mere
thought of them pained me. Had the mighty Julius appeared in
our schoolroom, he would have suffered the same fate that he
did in the Senate. When I had finished with such parts of his
'Gallic Wars' as we were made to read, I thought I had finished
with Caesar for good. And I mean for good.*

*Imagine, therefore, the incredulity with which I not long ago
found myself picking up, and not being able to put down, 'De
Bello Gallico' as newly translated by John Warrington. Mr.
Warrington admits he has taken liberties with the text. Instead
of a literal translation meant to help young students, he has
produced a version intended mainly for grown-ups who cannot read
Latin. He has not hesitated to 'elucidate obscurities by paraphrase',
to give all places when possible their present names, and to employ
the most modern English idioms to capture the vigor of the original. Furthermore, in the interest of vividness he has Caesar
write in the first person rather than the third, an alteration which
for the most part offers its obvious gains.*

*In spite of Mr. Warrington's slight but helpful revisions, it
is not 'De Bello Gallico' which has changed. It is we who come
back to it and the world in which we now read it that have
altered. The vocabulary of battle is nowadays on everyone's*

tongue. Most of us have had at least a wink at war and know a little from personal experience about the problems of combat, invasion, strategy, and logistics. No one brought up in the age of Mussolini, Hitler, Stalin, Malenkov, Franco, and Perón can have remained unschooled in the ways of dictators. Today we know, and gratefully recognize, the importance of able military leaders. We have read war books of every kind, including the memoirs of Eisenhower, Bradley, Wainwright, King, and Montgomery. We have had our proconsuls, too.

As a result, 'De Bello Gallico' has become a new book – tragically, stirringly contemporary. In Caesar's very first paragraph we are confronted with what we know as an 'Iron Curtain'. In the second, Lebensraum (in different terms) is encountered. By the third, mobilization and careful planning for Der Tag are reached. By the fourth paragraph we have met up with an informer, by the sixth the scorched earth policy, and by the eighth the blowing of a bridge. And so on page after page the parallels between past and present persist. We learn that Rome has been 'the victim of unprovoked aggression', and hear about reparations and hostages, satellite powers and secret agents, supply routes and the exchange of prisoners, the censorship of news and the fear of a peace conference being sabotaged, and even an attempt to isolate the Cherbourg Peninsula.

When in my youth I sweated my way through Caesar, my teacher, as far as I can recall, never mentioned that Napoleon, bent on destroying England, had assembled a fleet at Boulogne even as Caesar had for his second British expedition. Nowadays teachers, seeking quickening comparisons, would not have to go back so far in time. They have only to cite the barges Hitler vainly collected in the Channel or, better still, liken the armadas Caesar brought together for his attacks on Britain to the Normandy

Invasion. Certainly no one who participated in that invasion can read Caesar's account of the difficulties he faced without feeling a strange and exciting brotherhood over the centuries.

Were I a teacher hoping to make friends instead of enemies for Caesar's text, I would let my pupils make copious use of Mr. Warrington's translation. Before granting them this privilege, however, I would see to it that they had come to know something about Caesar, the man, by reading Shakespeare's tragedy, Shaw's 'Caesar and Cleopatra', Thornton Wilder's 'The Ides of March', and Plutarch's sketch. Thereafter I would lead them to the memoirs of Eisenhower, Bradley, and the rest (including Sherman and Grant). Then, and only then, would I permit them to feast upon Caesar. Perhaps they might enjoy his military narrative as much as I have recently (which is as much as I used to hate it), and come to realize that, as surely as 'what's past is prologue', what's present can be prologue to the past.

JOHN MASON BROWN

INTRODUCTION

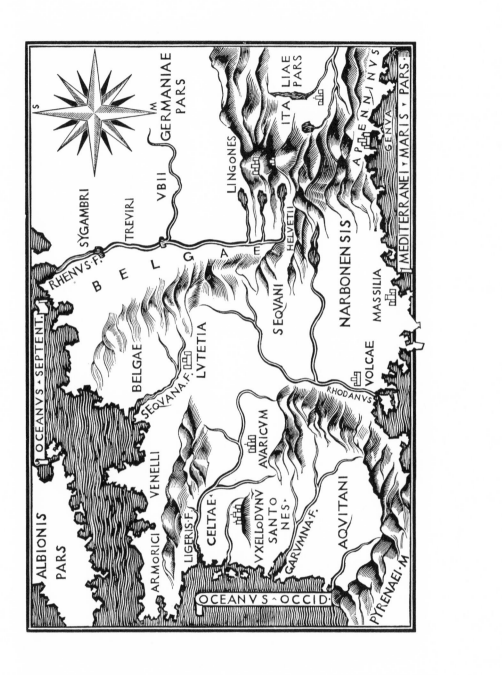

THE year 102 B.C., in which Gaius Julius Caesar was born,[1] was one of destiny. It was the year in which his uncle Marius, at the head of an army lately reorganized, annihilated the Teutones at Aix. It also inaugurated a period in the struggle between the popular and aristocratic parties, during which the interests of the republic yielded to the ambitions of a few powerful men, who, espousing the aims of political parties only to establish their own fortunes and authority, and relying upon armed force to achieve those ends, gave the final blow to a constitution already tottering to its fall.

The Social War (91-87 B.C.) was followed by the contest between Marius and Sulla, leaders respectively of the *populares* and *optimates*; and that bitter conflict (88-78) marked the beginning of more than half a century of civil strife. Sulla's dictatorship (81-79) ended temporarily the party struggles; but much of his constitution was abolished after his death, during a popular reaction led by Pompey and Crassus.

In the meantime Caesar had grown to manhood. According to Suetonius, whose account, though written perhaps one hundred and fifty years later, there seems no cause to doubt, Caesar was tall and pale, with full lips and dark piercing eyes. Scrupulous about his appearance, he attempted to conceal his premature baldness. He saw military service in Asia and Cilicia between 83 and 78, and was decorated for bravery at the storming of Mytilene under Minucius Thermus in 80. In that year also he was prominent among those who opposed the Sullan constitution; and in 77 he made his name at the Roman Bar, when he prosecuted Dolabella and established his reputation as an orator second only to Cicero.

In 68 he was quaestor in Spain; and in the following year Pompey left for the East, where for the next five years he conducted a number of successful campaigns, annexed Bithynia, Pontus, and Syria, and settled Judaea. During his term as aedile in 65 Caesar,

1. This is the most probable date, assigned by Mommsen. The traditional date is 100, and Carcopino argues for 101.

an avowed supporter of the *populares*, almost ruined himself by his prodigality in staging public games, and soon found himself indebted to Pompey's rival, the wealthy financier Marcus Licinius Crassus. In consequence of this association he was suspected of complicity in the first Catilinarian conspiracy; and in 63 he still further enraged the *optimates* by his election as pontifex maximus and by his planning, together with Crassus and at Pompey's expense, the agrarian measures which, proposed by the tribune Rullus, failed to become law owing to the vehement opposition of Cicero.

In 62 Pompey returned triumphant from the East, his sympathies no longer with the *populares*; but he disbanded his army, and thereby sacrificed an opportunity of establishing himself in power. The Senate, however, refused to provide land for his veterans or to ratify his Eastern settlement, and so alienated his support. Caesar meanwhile had served his term of office as praetor (62) and in 61 was governor of Further (i.e. Western) Spain, where he won a number of successes against the Lusitanians and made good his financial losses of four years earlier. Returning in 60, he asked leave of the Senate to stand for the consulate. Permission was refused. Accordingly, he formed with Pompey and Crassus the First Triumvirate in opposition to the Senate, secured the consulate for the year 59, and gave his daughter Julia[1] in marriage to Pompey.

The year 59 was one of the most momentous in the history of Western Europe, for it witnessed the *Lex Vatinia*, which conferred on Caesar, for five years as from March 58, the government of Cisalpine Gaul[2] and Illyricum, to which the Senate added Transalpine Gaul,[3] with four legions, a quaestor, and a staff of five (soon increased to ten) *legati*. He started for his province early in 58, and

1. Caesar married thrice: first, Cornelia, daughter of Lucius Cinna in 84; his refusal to divorce her on Sulla's orders nearly cost him his head. Second, Pompeia, Sulla's granddaughter, in 67; divorced in 61 as not 'above suspicion'. Third, Calpurnia, daughter of Lucius Piso Caesoninus, in 59. Julia was his daughter by Cornelia.
2. Northern Italy between the Alps and the Apennines.
3. Languedoc, Dauphiné, and Provence. After Caesar's conquests it included the whole area bounded by the Rhine, the Ocean, the Pyrénées, and the Mediterranean.

was soon engaged in that series of brilliant campaigns, of which he has left us an account in the *De Bello Gallico*. He used, however, to return for a period each year to Northern Italy after settling his troops in winter quarters; and on one such visit, in April 56, he met his colleagues at Lucca; the Triumvirate was renewed, and his own command extended for another five years as from 55 B.C. However, in 54 Julia died, and a year later Crassus was slain at Carrhae. The alliance of Pompey with Caesar, founded on personal interest and cemented only by a short-lived marriage, began quickly to dissolve. Both were ambitious: Pompey was jealous of his colleague's success in Gaul and of his renown as a commander in the field; nor did Caesar intend to lay down his office and risk the malice of his enemies. A crisis was at hand.

The conference of Lucca had conferred upon Pompey and Crassus the consulate for 55, and a five years' *imperium*[1] from that date. In 52 Pompey's *imperium* was prolonged for yet another five years. The senatorial party had determined to be revenged on Caesar, and constitutional arguments were adduced to cover the hatred that invariably follows superior intelligence and material success: for if Caesar was a threat to the republic, the republic was already in the throes of death, unequal to honest administration and unworthy of empire. A small clique, led by Marcus Porcius Cato, resolved that as soon as Caesar's command expired in November 49 they would prosecute him for treason or extortion. Now according to Roman law an interval of ten years was required to elapse between a consul's one term of office and the next. Caesar would therefore be entitled to stand for election in 49: if elected he would be legally immune from prosecution, and it was therefore decided to recall him before the expiry of his command. Pompey's support was indispensable to effect this measure, and it was urgently solicited. After temporizing throughout the years 51 and 50 he consented, and the die was cast. On the night of 11 January 49 B.C. Caesar crossed the Rubicon.

In his unfinished work, *De Bello Civili*, we have an account of

1. Supreme administrative power, including military command and right to interpret the laws. Pompey's province was Spain, but he governed by proxy.

those wonderful campaigns in Italy, Spain, Epirus, and the crown-
ing glory of Pharsalus, down to November 48. Having established
his mistress, Cleopatra, on the throne of Egypt, and defeated Phar-
naces of Pontus at Zela (47), he returned to Rome: but early next
year he went to Africa to meet a new threat from the combined
forces of Metellus Scipio and King Juba I of Numidia. They were
annihilated at Thapsus, after a campaign of only four months, and
Caesar celebrated four triumphs in honour of his Gallic, Alexan-
drian, Pontic, and African successes. The final struggle ended with
the victory at Munda, over the sons of Pompey and Labienus (45):
Caesar was master of the Roman world, emperor in all but name,
and the republic had passed away for ever. Less than a year later,
on the Ides of March 44 B.C., he lay murdered at the foot of
Pompey's statue.

We cannot enter here into Caesar's administration during the
brief period of his supremacy, for the Commentaries are concerned
almost exclusively with his military enterprises. Lucan has described him in a famous line:

Nil actum credens cum quid superesset agendum.

Endowed with marvellous energy of mind and body, he was
an able and astute politician; and his measures were conceived on
a popular basis with a certain breadth of view. Yet we must
hesitate to call him a statesman of the first rank: for there is evidence to suggest either that he aimed to make Rome a totalitarian
state, or that he was an opportunist – both signs of weakness rather
than of strength in the sphere of government.

2

THE military genius of Caesar, unsurpassed in the ancient world,
is evident upon every page of the Commentaries; and certain
questions will occur to the student of his campaigns, answers to
which are essential to a proper understanding of the nature and
the magnitude of his achievement.

First, then, as to the organization of Caesar's army, which was the main instrument of his rise to power. It was substantially the same as that instituted by Marius, who substituted voluntary enlistment for conscription on a property basis, and established an army more closely attached to, because more directly dependent upon, its commander-in-chief.

The largest military unit was the legion, normally consisting, though often much below strength, of 6,000 men in ten cohorts. The cohort of 600 men was the principal unit: it finds an almost exact modern equivalent in the battalion, and has been so translated in the following pages. Each cohort was made up of three maniples of two centuries apiece. On active service one or more cohorts might be detached for various duties. Enlistment was for twenty years; equipment was uniform; and pay was raised by Caesar from 120 denarii to 225 denarii a year, less a deduction for rations.

The legionary officers have no exact modern counterparts. The commander-in-chief (*imperator*) had (*a*) a quaestor, who combined the duties of chief of staff and quartermaster-general; (*b*) a staff (varying in number) of *legati*, of senatorial rank, whom, according to the context, I have described either as staff officers, officers of general rank, or legionary commanders. It was Caesar himself who first placed each legion under the immediate command of a *legatus*, though it should be noted that not every *legatus* was at all times so employed; (*c*) the *tribuni militum*, of equestrian rank, of whom there were six to each legion, were used by Caesar to command cohorts, groups of cohorts, and even ships. I have described them generally as battalion commanders; (*d*) under them were the centurions, officers who had risen from the ranks, and upon whom the general principally relied in battle; each of them commanded a century, so that there were 60 to the legion. The senior centurion, often mentioned by Caesar, was he who commanded the leading century in the first maniple of No. 1 cohort.

Attached to the legion were units of auxiliary horse and foot, recruited outside Italy and commanded by *praefecti*, some of whom were native officers. The cavalry was mainly from Germany, Gaul and Spain; the infantry were light-armed troops, e.g. slingers and archers.

The commander-in-chief was responsible not only for handling these units in camp, on the march, and on the battlefield. He had also to arrange his own commissariat and communications; he received no strategic directives from his government: and in place of maps he had to rely upon native guides. A perusal of Caesar's narrative reveals on the one hand that both he and his men had powers of physical endurance, which to-day may well appear incredible. It likewise proves his mastery in every branch of the science of war. The devotion of his troops is evident throughout, and his marvellous ability to handle soldiers under the most difficult and trying circumstances is perhaps nowhere better shown than at the siege of Bourges, and in the astonishing operations immediately after Pharsalus.

But if the loyalty and affection of his men were due mainly to his own personality and to his sincere interest in their welfare, that loyalty and affection were strengthened and confirmed by his success: for as he himself remarks, soldiers have no use for a failure. What then were Caesar's outstanding qualities in the field? Swiftness (*celeritas*) always and everywhere; discipline tempered with understanding of the fallible human element, but unbending towards cowardice and rebellion; clemency towards the defeated.

3

THE first seven books of the *De Bello Gallico* were probably written during the winter of 52-51 B.C. at Bibracte, and published early in the latter year. Caesar had not to rely entirely upon his memory, for he had access not only to his own private papers and his dispatches to the Senate, which were still extant when Suetonius wrote, but also to reports from his lieutenants and others. It is likewise possible that in such technical descriptions as those of the Rhine bridge he had the assistance of Lucius Cornelius Balbus, his chief engineer.

The structure of the Latin language and the Latin idiom do not lend themselves to what is generally called a literal translation. The long complicated sentences must be broken down, and some means must be found to deal with reported speech within reported speech. Briefly, the original must be rendered as faithfully as possible in our modern idiom. I have therefore endeavoured to present the Commentaries in the vigorous English of to-day.

Caesar, following a convention, and not because of any Olympian aloofness, wrote in the third person. I have allowed him to speak directly in the first person: the narrative becomes thereby more vivid, and difficulties in reported speech are overcome. As the version is intended mainly for those who cannot read Latin, I have not hesitated to elucidate obscurities by paraphrase. To avoid an excessive use of footnotes, I have given all units of money, weights, and measures their modern English equivalents in the text; and in order that the reader may not have constantly to refer to maps, I have given all places, when possible, their modern names, e.g. *Avaricum* – Bourges; *in finibus Haeduorum* (lit. in the territory of the Aedui) – in Burgundy. In such cases, however, the Latin appears, at least on the first occasion, in parentheses.

If the present volume is less helpful than a more 'literal' translation to young students in their efforts to construe, I will only say that such is not its primary purpose, and express at the same time a hope that its perusal may give life to what is too often made for them a lifeless task.

J. W.

BOOK ONE

[58 B.C.]

Geographical and Racial Divisions of Gaul

GAUL consists of three distinct regions, inhabited respectively by the Belgae, the Aquitani, and a people who call themselves Celts, but are known to us as Galli. The boundary between these latter and the Aquitani is the river Garonne, the Marne and Seine forming the Gallo-Belgic frontier. Variations in custom, language, and law distinguish these three peoples of whom the sturdiest are the Belgae. They are remote from the Roman Province, they have infrequent trade contacts with its high culture and refinement, and thus remain unaffected by influences which tend to effeminate character. They are, moreover, constantly at war with the Germans, whose country lies beyond the Rhine. Among the Galli no people is more formidable than the Helvetii: they too are engaged in almost ceaseless hostilities, offensive or defensive, against the Germans.

Conspiracy of Orgetorix

AT the time of which I write, by far the wealthiest and most distinguished of the Helvetii was a man named Orgetorix, the goal of whose consuming ambition was nothing less than supreme power. In the consulship of Messala and Piso [61 B.C.] he conspired with his fellow chieftains and persuaded the whole people to migrate. He argued

3

that with their superior military skill they could make short
work of subjugating the whole of Gaul; and his induce-
ments were the more acceptable because of the narrow
geographical limits of their territory. On one side a great
river, the Rhine, barred them from Germany; on another
the lofty Jura range stood between them and the Sequani;
and they were cut off on a third side from the Roman
Province by the Lake of Geneva and the Rhône. In these
circumstances their movements were restricted. To launch
an attack across their frontiers was no easy matter, a fact
which proved a most irksome restraint upon this warlike
people; and although their territory measured 227 by 170
miles, they considered that small in relation to their large
population and their high military renown.

The weight of these arguments and the personal influence
of Orgetorix were decisive; the Helvetii determined to
mobilize. Their plans included the buying up of all available wagons and pack-animals, the sowing of crops on the
widest possible scale to ensure an adequate corn supply on
the march, and the establishment of friendly relations with
neighbouring states. They calculated that two years would
suffice for these preliminaries, and their departure was of-
ficially decreed for the third year.

Orgetorix was appointed to supervise the arrangements,
and he undertook in person an embassy to the states. In the
course of this journey he incited a Sequanian named Cas-
ticus (whose father had for many years governed that tribe
with the title of 'Friend' conferred by the Senate) to usurp
royal authority. His next move, supported by the gift of his
own daughter in marriage, was a proposal that Dumnorix
should attempt a similar coup against his brother Divitiacus, the popular chieftain of the Aedui. He assured both
these men that the scheme was simplicity itself: he meant

4

to seize the government of the all-powerful Helvetii, and having done so, would use his own resources and his own troops to confirm them in authority. On the strength of these guarantees they exchanged solemn pledges, looking forward to the day when they would unite in the conquest of Gaul at the head of three powerful and determined nations.

The Helvetii learned of this conspiracy through an informer, and according to custom Orgetorix had to stand his trial in chains; if the verdict were 'Guilty' the penalty was death by fire. On the day fixed for the hearing he assembled every one of his 10,000 vassals, and they, together with numerous dependants and retainers, were gathered at the court. A trial was thus avoided. The people, however, were furious: they determined to assert their right by force of arms, and the magistrates were actually collecting a large body of men from the countryside when Orgetorix was found dead. According to the Helvetii there was some suspicion of suicide.

Migration of the Helvetii: Roman Countermeasures

PLANS for the migration, however, went on despite the death of Orgetorix; and an alliance was made with the Boii, who had left their homes across the Rhine, entered Noricum, and were at that time besieging Noreia. When at last the Helvetii considered themselves sufficiently prepared, each man was ordered to take with him three months' supply of flour, and the rest of the grain was burned together with their twelve towns, four hundred villages, and all their country houses. The same course was followed by their near neighbours the Rauraci, Tulingi, and Latobrigi, who had been persuaded to join the exodus.

There was method in all this: for by making it impossible to turn back they ensured a greater readiness to face the trials that lay ahead.

There was a choice of only two routes by which the Helvetii could leave their country. One of these, the Pas de l'Écluse (*unum*), led through the dominions of the Sequani; but it was a narrow and difficult pass between the Jura and the Rhône, scarcely wide enough for the passage of wagons in single file, and dominated by a towering cliff which would enable a handful of men to hold the road against them. The other route lay through the Roman Province: it was much easier and relatively free from obstacles. The Rhône can be forded at certain points, and at the border town of Geneva it was crossed by a bridge giving access to Helvetian territory. Immediately beyond the river lay Savoy, where the Allobroges had recently been subdued, and were presumed as yet to have little good-will towards Rome. The Helvetii were therefore confident of obtaining a passage through their territory, by force of arms if not by negotiation. Their arrangements were now complete, and they fixed a date for their assembly on the banks of the Rhône: that date was 28 March in the consul-ship of Piso and Gabinius.

I was in Rome when news reached me that these people were attempting to move through the Province. I left for Transalpine Gaul at once and hurried to Geneva, where I gave orders for general mobilization and had the bridge destroyed. The Helvetii heard of my arrival and sent a deputation of notables led by Nammeius and Verucloetius. They insisted that they meant to do no harm on the march, but that as there was no alternative route they sought leave to move through the Province. Now, it was a canton of the Helvetii (the Tigurini, to be exact) who defeated Lu-

6

cius Cassius [109 B.C.], slew the consul himself, and sent the remnants of his army under the yoke. With that in mind I decided that their request must be refused: they were a hostile people, and it was unlikely they would refrain from violence if once allowed to pass. On the other hand, I was anxious to gain time until mobilization was complete, and therefore told the envoys that my reply would have to be deferred; they might, if they so wished, return on 13 April.

Meanwhile my one legion and some new recruits threw up an eighteen-mile line of earthworks between Geneva and the Jura. These fortifications were 16 feet high, and had strongly built redoubts manned by pickets. Their purpose was to facilitate our resistance should the enemy prove defiant and attempt to cross the river.

In due course the deputation returned, and I told them that I could not, consistently with Roman custom and precedent, grant any one a passage through the Province. I also made it clear that, if necessary, I would meet force with force.

Their plans had thus gone wrong, and they now tried storming their way over: there were sporadic daylight attacks, but operations were carried on mainly under cover of darkness, some using a bridge of boats, others relying on the fords wherever the stream was fairly shallow. But our earthworks, strong troop concentrations, and heavy fire were too much for them, and they finally abandoned the attempt.

Intrigues of Dumnorix

ONLY one route now remained, the Pas de l'Écluse; but it was hopeless unless the Sequani agreed, being much too narrow. The Helvetii failed to negotiate a passage, and sent representatives to Dumnorix asking him to use his good offices with the Sequani and obtain their permission. Now this man Dumnorix had a good deal of influence with the Sequani because of his personal charm and generosity. He was friendly with the Helvetii also, having married a lady of that tribe, the daughter of Orgetorix. He was extremely ambitious, and, with revolution already in mind, was only too glad to have as many states as possible bound to himself by ties of gratitude. Accordingly he undertook the mission, and prevailed upon the Sequani to allow the migrant host a passage through their country. He likewise negotiated an exchange of hostages whereby the Sequani undertook not to molest the Helvetii, who agreed in turn to do no damage on their march.

Roman Offensive

I DISCOVERED that the Helvetii were proposing to move through the southern Jura and Beaujolais westward into Périgord (*per agrum Sequanorum et Haeduorum . . . in Santonum fines*). This was not far from the borders of Toulouse, an open and very fertile district within the Roman Province; and it was evident that if the Helvetii reached their goal we should be confronted with a dangerous situation. I therefore appointed Titus Labienus to command during my absence, and hurried to Italy. There I raised two new legions, summoned another three from winter quarters around Aquileia, and with these five took the shortest route back to Transalpine Gaul. In the mountainous region of the Alps the combined forces of the Ceutrones, Graioceli, and Caturiges tried to intercept us. There was some heavy fighting, but they were driven off; and seven days after leaving Oulx (*ab Ocelo*) in the extreme west of Cisalpine Gaul we reached Dauphiny (*in fines Vocontiorum*). From there we made our way north-west (*ab Allobrogibus*) and halted near Lyons (*in Segusiavos*), immediately beyond the Rhône. The Helvetii had by this time emerged from the Pas de l'Écluse, crossed the Plateau de Dombes (*per . . . fines Sequanorum*), and entered Beaujolais (*in Haeduorum fines*), which they had begun to pillage. The Aedui could

do nothing to defend themselves or their property, and sent envoys to ask for our assistance. They claimed always to have deserved well of Rome, and argued that it was unfair that a Roman army should stand by and watch the devastation of their farmlands, the sack of their towns, and the deportation of their children into slavery. At the same time the Ambarri, who were closely related to the Aedui, informed me that their country had been ravaged, and they were now finding it hard to defend their towns against enemy attack. Finally the Allobroges arrived in consternation: they had at one time owned villages and other possessions beyond the Rhône, but now, so they told me, they had lost all but their empty fields.

It seemed, in the circumstances, advisable to act before the Helvetii had destroyed all the resources of our allies and reached Périgord (*in Santonos*).

The Saône is a tributary of the Rhône, flowing through

southern Burgundy and the Mâconnais (*per fines Haeduorum et Sequanorum*) so sluggishly that one cannot at first glance tell the direction of its course. The Helvetii were in the act of crossing this river by boat and a bridge of rafts when scouts reported that although three of their cantons were over, a fourth, the Tigurini, were still on the left bank. A little after midnight I started from camp with three legions, came up with them unprepared and encumbered with luggage, and annihilated a large part of their force. The remainder fled for refuge into some neighbouring woods. It was, as I have said, this very tribe which, on a lone expedition about fifty years ago, had inflicted a crushing defeat on Cassius. Thus, either by chance or by divine providence, the first of the Helvetii to expiate this disaster to our arms were those by whom it had been inflicted. Incidentally, too, I satisfied a private grudge as well as avenging a public calamity, for among those who fell with Cassius was Lucius Piso, his second in command and my wife's great-grandfather.

The next objective was to engage the main Helvetian army. A bridge was thrown over the Saône, and the army crossed. The enemy were demoralized by our sudden and unexpected arrival, for we had succeeded in getting over the river in a single day, a feat which they had only just managed in twenty. They sent a deputation headed by Divico, who had commanded them in the campaign against Cassius, and the following is an outline of his remarks:

If Rome would make peace, the Helvetii would settle in any district I might care to name; but if I were going to persist in hostilities I would do well to remember a previous Roman misfortune and the age-long valour of his people. Certainly I had caught one canton unawares; but they had been off their guard at a moment when their comrades had crossed the river and could do nothing to help them. I must not, therefore, exaggerate my own strength or underrate theirs: the Helvetii had learned from their fathers to rely upon courage rather than cunning in warfare. He concluded by warning me not to adopt a course which must end in the annihilation of a Roman army and thereby make that place of our meeting a byword for all time at Rome.

I replied that the incidents to which they had referred made me the less inclined to modify my intention: Rome had been the victim of unprovoked aggression. Had she been a conscious aggressor, she could without difficulty have taken steps to prevent retaliation; as it was, she had been misled precisely because she had no recollection of having acted in any way deserving of reprisals, and had therefore felt no cause for anxiety. Even were I prepared to forget bygone insults, it was quite impossible to over-look these latest affronts. First there was the attempt to force a way through the Roman Province in defiance of my order; then their ill treatment of the Aedui, Ambarri, and Allobroges. They might boast of their glorious victory and of having for so long escaped retribution for their crimes; yet both those facts led to one conclusion: when the immortal gods mean to punish guilty man they often grant him all the more prosperity, all the longer impunity, simply that he may suffer the more when his good fortune is reversed. However, I expressed myself willing to make peace on condition that they gave hostages against the ful-filment of their promises, and made restitution for the damage done to the Aedui, the Allobroges, and their allies.

Divico's answer was that, in accordance with their ancient traditions, the Helvetii received hostages, but surrendered none: Rome knew that only too well. He then withdrew.

Next day the Helvetii struck camp, and we did the same. Our cavalry, which amounted to some 4,000 men recruited from all parts of the Province, and included some of the Aedui and their allies, went ahead to reconnoitre the enemy's line of march; but they were rather too keen in their pursuit, engaged his rearguard cavalry on unfavourable ground, and suffered some casualties. The natives were tremendously excited over the repulse of this large body of cavalry by a mere 500 horsemen. They halted their column, and tried by sporadic attacks from the rear to make us re-engage. I refused to be drawn: it appeared sufficient for the time being to prevent them scouring the countryside for plunder and forage; and so the march continued for about a fortnight with never more than five or six miles between our vanguard and their rear.

Further Schemes of Dumnorix

MEANWHILE I was continually pressing the Aedui for the grain which they had contracted to supply. In these cold northern latitudes the standing corn was not yet ripe; we had insufficient stocks, and were even short of fodder. I had arranged for a certain amount of corn to be brought up the Saône by boat; but it was not at the moment available, as the Helvetii had struck off from the river, and I was unwilling to discontinue our pursuit. The Aedui put me off from day to day: it was being collected, they said; brought in; on the way. They clearly meant to delay indefinitely, and in a very short while the troops were due to draw their rations.

We had in camp a number of Aeduan chiefs among whom were Divitiacus and a man named Liscus, their principal magistrate, an officer elected annually with the official style of Vergobret and invested with powers of life and death. I called a meeting of those chiefs and rated them for their lack of co-operation at this crucial time with the enemy so near and no grain to be bought or harvested. I emphasized that it was largely in response to their own appeals that the campaign had been undertaken at all. Liscus was driven by these strictures to disclose something about which he had until then kept silent. There were certain influential persons, he said, more powerful in a private capacity than the authorities themselves: these individuals, with their bombastic and seditious talk, were urging the population to withhold the promised supplies. Their argument was that, since the conquest of Gaul was now out of the question, it was better to submit to the government of fellow Gauls than to the authority of Rome. They were saying that once Rome had subdued the Helvetii she would undoubtedly impose her rule on the Aedui and every one else besides. These same persons were handing on all our plans to the enemy, and keeping them informed of everything that went on in our camp. He himself could do nothing to stop them; he had felt obliged to make these facts known, but had done so at great personal risk, and had therefore remained silent as long as he possibly could.

I had a feeling that the reference was to Divitiacus's brother Dumnorix. Not wishing, however, to discuss the matter before so many people, I broke up the meeting but detained Liscus and questioned him privately as to his remarks. He answered quite readily and straightforwardly; and after some further secret inquiries my suspicions were confirmed: Dumnorix was the culprit.

It appeared that he was a self-assured type, highly esteemed by his own people because of his open-handedness, and a revolutionary into the bargain. For several years he had held a contract for all the Aeduan taxes, including river tolls, and had obtained that contract at a very low figure because no one dared oppose his bid. In this way he had amassed a fortune, and had also raised considerable sums earmarked for bribery. At his own expense he maintained a large force of household cavalry in constant attendance on his person, and to strengthen his already dominant influence at home and abroad he had given his own mother in marriage to the most eminent chieftain of the Bituriges. He had likewise disposed of his half-sister and other female relatives among various neighbouring states; and as his wife was a Helvetian, he was also an active supporter of that people.

It transpired further that he hated Rome, and myself in particular on personal grounds; for our arrival had lessened his authority and confirmed Divitiacus in his honours and dignities. He presumed that in the event of a Roman defeat the Helvetii would help him to the throne, whereas under Roman government he despaired not only of the kingly title but even of his present influence.

There was something else too. Dumnorix commanded the Aeduan horse, a part of our auxiliary forces; and when investigating the failure of the recent cavalry skirmish I discovered that the first to turn tail, and thereby spread panic in face of quite a small enemy troop, were Dumnorix and his contingent.

To the damning evidence of these revelations were added other undeniable facts. It was Dumnorix who brought the Helvetii through the Pas de l'Écluse and arranged an exchange of hostages. He had acted without orders from me, and the Aeduan authorities were complaining that he had done so without any instructions from them: indeed they had been ignorant of the whole proceeding. In the circumstances there appeared good grounds for dealing with him myself or for asking his government to do so. One thing, however, made me hesitate. I had come to realize the very high regard which his brother Divitiacus entertained for Rome and his personal devotion to me. He was a man of unswerving loyalty, with a strong sense of justice and moderate views, and there was a possibility that the execution of his brother might alienate his goodwill. So before taking further steps I sent for Divitiacus and dispensed with the official interpreters. The conversation took place through the medium of Gaius Valerius Procillus, a distinguished provincial, who was an intimate friend of his, a man in whom he had complete confidence. After reminding him of the charges against his brother to which he had listened in the council, I told him of certain other things which I had gathered from private sources. Then, coming to the point, I said: 'Please don't take offence at this; but I'm going to ask your consent to my dealing with the case in person, or else to my instructing your government to take action.'

Divitiacus burst into tears: with abject humility he began imploring me not to pass too heavy a sentence on his brother. He admitted the truth of the accusations, and protested that no one was more sorry about it than himself. In the heyday of his power he had been responsible for his brother's advancement, a helpless youth who had afterwards used every possible means to undermine his influence, and had nearly brought about his ruin. He went on, however, to plead the cause of brotherly love and public opinion. He argued that in the event of my taking extreme measures no one would believe him innocent of complicity—it would seem to follow inevitably from our close friendship—and the whole of Gaul would be estranged.

By way of ending this tearful harangue, I took his hand and told him not to worry: because of my high regard for him his prayer should be granted, and the insult to Rome as well as my personal grievance forgiven. Dumnorix was then brought in and confronted with his brother. He heard a list of his crimes based on my investigations and the complaints of his own people. I warned him that he owed his pardon solely to his brother's intervention, and he must give no further cause for suspicion. Nevertheless, I set agents to keep an eye on him, and to let me know his movements and with whom he corresponded.

Abortive Operations at Sanvinge

On the same day it was reported by scouts that the enemy had halted eight miles away. They had encamped at the foot of a hill, the ascent of which was found on reconnaissance to present no difficulty. I therefore went over plans with Labienus, and ordered him to proceed to the summit shortly after midnight with two legions guided by the patrol which had just inspected the route. An hour or so after his departure I sent the entire cavalry corps ahead and started out along the road which the enemy had taken. Our forward patrols were commanded by Publius Considius who was supposed to be an experienced officer, having served under both Sulla and Crassus. Labienus had reached his objective before dawn, and I was by that time within one and a half miles of the Helvetian camp. Subsequent information obtained from prisoners revealed that the Gauls were quite unaware of our approach, when Considius arrived at the gallop with news that the hill was in enemy hands: he had recognized their armour and crests. I immediately drew off the troops towards a nearby height and deployed for battle.

Now in order to ensure a simultaneous attack, Labienus

16

had been instructed not to engage until he saw the main force closing in on the enemy's position. Having occupied the ridge, he was awaiting our approach; and it was quite late in the day when patrols reported that we had been all along in possession of the heights and that the Helvetii were again on the move. Considius had simply lost his nerve and reported having seen what in fact he had not seen at all. For the rest of the day, therefore, we followed at the usual distance, and halted three miles from the enemy's encampment.

There were now only forty-eight hours before the troops were to draw their rations, and something had to be done to obtain supplies. We were no more than sixteen miles from Bibracte, the largest and best-stocked Aeduan stronghold, so I broke off the pursuit and made for that place. The news was carried to the Helvetii by some deserters from Aemilius's Gallic horse; and, in view of our failure the day before to use our advantage and attack, the Helvetii may have been under the impression that we were retreating in alarm. Perhaps they merely felt confident of cutting us off from supplies; but whatever the reason, they altered their plan, switched their line of march, and began to follow and harass our rear.

Battle of Col d'Armecy

REALIZING what was afoot, I drew off my forces to the nearest high ground, and sent the cavalry to meet their attack. Meanwhile the four veteran legions were formed in triple line half-way up the hill; the two newly conscripted legions with the whole auxiliary force were posted on the summit. The entire height above was thus covered with troops, and these men in the upper line were ordered to

17

entrench the packs and heavy equipment which had been
stacked together. The Helvetii had followed with all their
baggage loaded on carts, with which they now formed
a stockade on some rising ground.

In very close order they proceeded to hurl back the
cavalry, and then came on in mass formation against our
front line. I had my own horse and then all officers' mounts
moved out of sight so as to equalize every one's peril and
leave no one any chance of escape. To encourage the troops,
I issued a verbal order of the day, and then joined battle.

The legionaries, with the advantage of higher ground,
easily smashed the enemy's formation with a volley of
pikes, and having thus thrown it into confusion drew their
swords and charged. The Gallic line was now in serious
difficulties: our pikes had in many cases pierced through
several shields at once and locked them together. The iron
had been bent, and they could neither withdraw it nor
fight properly with the left arm thus engaged. Many of

them tried for some time to shake themselves free, but in
the end preferred to drop their shields and fight with no
body protection. Exhausted by their casualties, they eventually began to fall back on a hill rather less than a mile
distant. We followed up; but no sooner had they reached

their objective, than the Boii and Tulingi attacked: numbering some 15,000 men, they had closed the enemy's column and formed his rearguard. Turning on our advancing right flank, they prepared to take it from behind; and as soon as the Helvetii saw this development they launched a counter-attack.

We formed into two divisions: the first two lines to oppose that section of the enemy which had already been checked and driven back, the third to meet these newcomers.

The action was now fought on two fronts, and after some time the enemy was no longer able to stand his ground. Part of his forces began once more to retire on the hill while the rest concentrated on the stockade. The engagement had lasted from midday till evening, and during all that time not one man was seen to turn and run. Fighting at the stockade went on far into the night: the enemy kept up a steady fire, and as our troops advanced uphill they suffered some casualties from native weapons discharged through the wheels by men crouching beneath the wagons. After a prolonged struggle, however, we captured their transport, and also their encampment, where Orgetorix's daughter and one of his sons were taken prisoner.

Surrender of the Helvetii

THE enemy survivors numbered about 130,000: they marched all that night, and three days later reached Lingonian territory in the Côte d'Or (*in fines Lingonum*). We had not been able to follow, because a three days' delay was necessary in order to tend the wounded and bury our dead; but I sent couriers with letters to the Lingones, forbidding them to assist with supplies or otherwise, and threatening, if they did, to regard them on a level with the Helvetii. When the three days were up we resumed the chase in full strength.

The Helvetii were now destitute, and were therefore obliged to send envoys to negotiate a surrender: they met me on the road, grovelled, and begged for peace. They were directed to halt their column and remain where they were. The order was obeyed. I arrived in due course and demanded hostages, their arms, and our slaves who had deserted to them. While a search was made for these fugitives and the arms were being collected, night fell, and some 6,000 men of a canton known as Verbigene managed to leave the Helvetian camp, and made a dash for the German frontier on the Rhine. They may have been scared at the prospect of being slaughtered once they had been disarmed; or they may simply have been tempted by the opportunity, and imagined that in so vast a crowd of prisoners their own flight could be concealed for a time or even go quite unnoticed. But as soon as the facts were reported I ordered the inhabitants of those districts through which they passed to round them up and bring them back, unless they themselves wished to be considered accessories. Brought back they were, and dealt with accordingly.

As for the remainder, when they had delivered hostages and handed over their arms and the deserters, their surrender was accepted. The Helvetii, Tulingi, and Latobrigi were ordered back to their respective territories; but having lost all the produce of their lands, they were faced with certain starvation on their return. I therefore directed the Allobroges to supply them with grain, but insisted that they themselves must rebuild their towns and villages. I was particularly anxious that the territory abandoned by the Helvetii should not be left unpopulated: it was rich land,

and might lure the Germans across the Rhine, with the result that we should then have them as neighbours of the Allobroges and our Gallic province.

The Aedui asked to be allowed to settle the Boii in their country, and I granted their request. These Boii are a remarkably brave race; they were allotted farmlands, and, at a later date, admitted to equal status with their hosts in rights and liberty.

I was shown some lists, written in Greek characters, which were found in the Helvetian camp: they proved to be numerical registers of the emigrant host. Those of military age, children, old men, women, were all recorded separately, tribe by tribe. The figures were as follows:

Helvetii	263,000
Tulingi	36,000
Latobrigi	14,000
Rauraci	23,000
Boii	32,000
	368,000

Men able to bear arms numbered 92,000, and a census of those who returned home showed a total of 110,000.

Operations against the Helvetii were now ended, and chieftains representing states over a large area of Gaul assembled to offer their congratulations. They recognized that the campaign had avenged injuries which Rome had suffered from the Helvetii in the past, but they considered that Gaul had profited no less than Rome by the event. The Helvetii, they said, had migrated on the flood-tide of prosperity with the express purpose of making general war and of establishing their rule over the whole of Gaul. They had intended to choose—and the choice was sufficiently wide—the most convenient and most fertile areas for their own domain, and to make the rest of the states their tributaries.

The deputies then sought leave to proclaim a general council of the Gauls on a date to be decided, and to announce that they did so with my consent. They had certain requests to submit, but desired first to reach general agreement among themselves. Permission was given: they fixed a date for their assembly, but swore on oath that none except those unanimously authorized would disclose its proceedings.

Ariovistus

WHEN the council was over the same chieftains returned and asked me to meet them privately for secret discussions upon a matter which, they said, touched their personal safety and the public welfare. The audience was granted. On their knees, and in great distress, they assured me that, anxious as they were to obtain their request, they were equally concerned to make sure that no word of what they were going to say should leak out: otherwise they foresaw themselves victims of a terrible revenge.

Divitiacus then acted as their spokesman. He explained that Gaul was for many years split into two factions, led respectively by the Aedui and Arverni. They had contested the supremacy with extreme bitterness until, at last, the Arverni and Sequani [71 B.C.] had purchased German intervention. In the first instance about 15,000 of these savage mercenaries had crossed the Rhine. They began, after a time, to appreciate the Gallic farmlands and the Gallic way of life; and then they brought over others, until there were now about 120,000 of them in Gaul. The Aedui and their dependent states had made stubborn resistance; but defeat had brought disaster in its train, and they had lost all their

22

most prominent men, the whole of their national council, and the flower of their army. These calamities had in turn shattered the paramount power they had once enjoyed in Gaul, thanks to their native valour and the Roman alliance. They had been obliged to surrender to the Sequani their leading citizens as hostages; they had been forced to give a solemn undertaking to require no hostages in return, to ask no aid from Rome, and to submit themselves permanently to the dictates of the conqueror. 'I alone,' said Divitiacus, 'of all my people would not agree to take the oath or give up my children. I fled, and went to Rome to solicit help from the Senate: I was the one man bound by neither oath nor hostages.'

He went on to describe how the victorious Sequani had nevertheless suffered a worse fate than the vanquished Aedui. The German king Ariovistus had settled in their territory and had seized a third of their farmlands, the finest land in Gaul. He had just ordered them to evacuate another third to make room for 24,000 Harudes who had joined him some months earlier. In a few years' time they would all be driven from Gaul, and the entire German nation would cross the Rhine; for there could be no comparison between the Gallic and German lands, nor between their respective standards of living. Ariovistus had won a single victory over the Gallic forces [60 B.C.] at Magetobriga, and was now exercising a brutal tyranny, demanding as hostages the children of every man of rank, and visiting them with the worst forms of torture unless everything followed at once on the least hint of his good pleasure. He was a savage, passionate and reckless, and his rule was no longer tolerable.

Divitiacus insisted that if the Gauls were left without the protection of Rome—which only I could give—they would have to follow the example of the Helvetii and migrate in search of a new home, new lands remote from the Germans, and chance whatever fate might befall them. If Ariovistus got to hear of all this he would undoubtedly take a most dreadful revenge upon the hostages already in his hands. He could, however, be overawed: my own authority and my army's reputation, the news of our recent victory, the very name of Rome, would prevent the introduction of a yet greater horde of Germans and protect the whole of Gaul from his oppression.

At the conclusion of this address there was loud lamentation, and they began all together to implore my help. It was noticeable, however, that the Sequani alone did not join in, but stood gazing sadly at the floor. I was surprised, and asked them the reason. There was no answer: they remained gloomy and silent, nor did repeated questioning elicit a word until Divitiacus again took up the tale. The Sequani, he said, were in a more unfortunate and more difficult position than the rest: they were frightened to complain or to ask for assistance, even in private. True, Ariovistus was a long way off; yet they trembled at the thought of his cruelty as if they were in his very presence. Others had at least a chance of escape, but the Sequani had Ariovistus in their midst: he had occupied all their towns, and they must suffer all his torments.

Caesar's Attempt to Negotiate

THAT is what I learned from the Gauls, and I put them in better spirits with a promise to give the matter careful consideration. I told them I had every hope that by a courteous show of authority I could persuade Ariovistus to abandon his evil courses; the meeting then broke up.

There were, in fact, a number of other reasons urging me to give the affair my attention and to take some action. In the first place the Senate had often addressed the Aedui as 'friends and brethren'; yet here were these people, slaves at the mercy of the Germans, and their hostages in the hands of Ariovistus and the Sequani. That seemed a grave reflection upon myself and upon the majesty of Rome. Again, it was evident that the Germans were gradually making a habit of crossing the Rhine, and the arrival of a large body of them in Gaul was a danger to Rome. It seemed improbable that these wild barbarians would simply occupy Gaul and then stop short: they were far more likely to do as the Cimbri and Teutones had done before them [102 and 101 B.C.]; they would break into the Province, and from there push on into Italy. It was clearly essential to face up to the situation without a moment's delay. As for Ariovistus, his overweening arrogance could certainly not be tolerated.

I therefore decided to send envoys asking him to name some intermediate point for a conference, as I wished to discuss with him affairs of State, matters of the greatest importance to us both. Ariovistus replied to the deputation: 'If I wanted anything of Caesar, I would go to him: if Caesar wants anything of me, he should come to me.' He went on to say that without an army he would not venture into any part of Roman-occupied Gaul, and he could not assemble an army without heavy expense and a deal of trouble. He was, moreover, at a loss to understand what business I personally or the Roman people at large might have in Gaul, which was his by right of conquest. On receipt of this answer I sent a second deputation, and the following is the text of my note:

You have been treated with the utmost courtesy by myself and the Roman Government: it was in my consulship that the Senate granted you the style of 'King and Friend'. In return, you make difficulties when invited to a conference, and treat the discussion of matters affecting both sides as no concern of yours.

I have, therefore, to request: (a) That you bring no more Germans across the Rhine into Gaul. (b) That you restore the Aeduan hostages at present held by you, and allow the Sequani complete freedom to do the same. (c) That you do nothing to provoke the Aedui, and refrain from hostilities against them and their allies. Subject to the fulfilment of these conditions, I myself and the Roman Government will entertain towards you continuing goodwill and friendship. But I must point out that in the consulship of Marcus Messala and Marcus Piso it was decreed by the Senate [61 B.C.] that the governor of the Gallic Province should protect the Aedui and other allies of Rome, consistently with the interests of the republic. Accordingly in the event of your failure to comply with my request, I shall not disregard the wrongs suffered by the Aedui.

The following is Ariovistus's reply:

The rules of war provide that the victor may dictate his own terms to the vanquished. Rome has always governed conquered peoples at her discretion, not at the orders of a third party. I give Rome no instructions how to exercise her rights: she has no business, then, to interfere with mine.

The Aedui risked war: they fought, and were defeated. Now, in consequence, they are tributaries. Your own arrival, incidentally, has done me grave harm by causing a reduction of my revenues. I shall not restore the Aeduan hostages.

So long as the Aedui stand by their agreement and pay their annual taxes, I shall not make war on them or their allies without cause. If they do not, then, I assure you, their title 'Brethren of the Romans' will do them little good. You declare that you will 'not disregard the wrongs suffered by the Aedui'. I may say that no one ever opposed me without involving himself in ruin. For fourteen years my Germans have not known a roof over their

26

heads: they are past masters in the science of war. Enter the lists when you choose, and learn the extent of their unconquerable might.

Occupation of Besançon: Panic in the Roman Army

No sooner had I received this missive than deputations arrived from the Aedui and the Treveri. The former came to protest against the pillage of their territory by the Harudes, who had lately crossed into Gaul: they had failed to buy peace from Ariovistus, even with the surrender of additional hostages. The Treveri reported that a hundred Suebian cantons under Nasua and Cimerius had encamped on the far bank of the Rhine, and were trying to cross the river. This was indeed grave news, and the time-factor appeared now all important. If this horde managed to effect a junction with Ariovistus's veteran troops, it might be rather difficult to oppose them. So, after making some hurried arrangement for food supplies, I began a series of forced marches to intercept Ariovistus.

We had been three days on the road when I was informed that the German commander was heading in full strength and at great speed for Besançon (*Vesontio*), the strongest fortress in that area (*Sequanorum*). His occupation of Besançon had to be prevented at all costs: the place was an arsenal; its natural defences, too, would make it an ideal point from which to prolong a campaign. It is almost completely encircled by the river Doubs in a line that might have been traced with compasses. The river leaves a gap of exactly 1,600 feet, but this is closed by a great hill, the base of which touches the banks on either side; and the hill itself is surrounded by a wall which makes it a fortress on its own and joins it to the town.

By marching day and night and forcing the pace I man-

27

aged to occupy Besançon. After stationing a garrison there we delayed for a few days in the neighbourhood to await food convoys and other supplies. Meanwhile the troops began questioning local people and foreign merchants, who regaled them with stories about the enormous stature of the Germans, their unbelievable courage and incredible military skill. They even told how, when they had chanced to meet them, they had often been unable to endure the gaze of those piercing eyes! The result was panic: the whole army was seized with mortal fear, and was almost insane with terror. It began with the sinecure officers of the legions and auxiliary corps and others holding mere honorary commissions—men with no military experience.

Some of these fellows began asking for leave on various pretexts, all of which, I was given to understand, were most urgent. Others had some sense of shame, and were anxious to avoid suspicion of cowardice; but though they remained, they could not disguise their looks nor, occasionally, their open distress. In the privacy of their tents they lamented their own fate, or sat with their friends deploring the general situation. All over the camp there was much signing and sealing of wills. This cowardly murmuring gradually had its effect even upon hardened troops—legionaries, centurions, cavalry commanders, all alike. A certain number were unwilling to show their alarm: they said it was not the enemy they feared, but they were worried over the narrow roads, the huge forests that lay between ourselves and the enemy, or a possible lack of proper transport for the food supplies. Some went so far as to tell me bluntly that, when the order was given to strike camp and proceed, the troops would not obey: they would be too scared to move.

As soon as I heard this, an officers' meeting was summoned, and centurions of all grades were ordered to attend.

After reprimanding them severely for daring to dispute or even to question the why and wherefore of their destination, I pointed out that during my consulship Ariovistus had been extremely anxious for Roman favour, and there was no reason to suppose he would now be so rash as to go back on his obligations: personally I was quite confident that when our demands were made known and the fairness of our terms properly understood, my own goodwill and that of Rome herself would carry some weight.

Suppose, however, that his fanaticism drove him to war: there was still nothing to fear; they could surely rely on their own spirit and my competence. The enemy was one of whom we had already taken the measure: a generation ago, when Marius defeated the Cimbri and Teutones, it was agreed that the troops had shared the honours equally with their commander. More recently there was the Servile War [73-71 B.C.] in Italy,[1] and on that occasion the slaves had in their favour a certain amount of Roman training and discipline. It was clear, then, that resolution was what counted: an enemy, armed and on the tide of victory, had been routed by men in whose eyes they had, though as yet unarmed, long been objects of unfounded dread. Another case in point was that of the Helvetii. At home or abroad, these people had been frequently in conflict with the Germans, and had generally come out on top: but the Helvetii themselves had proved no match for our forces.

If any one were disturbed by the Gallic defeat and subsequent collapse, an explanation of that was not far to seek. The Gauls had been exhausted by a long campaign: Ariovistus had for months lurked in his camp among the marshes, allowing them no opportunity to come to grips

---

1. The rebels included numerous Germans.

with him, until at last they had abandoned hope of ever doing so, and had dispersed. It was then that Ariovistus suddenly attacked: his victory was due rather to careful planning
than to fighting qualities. Planning, I argued, had served
against simple natives; but not even Ariovistus could
imagine his tactics capable of ensnaring the armies of Rome.

I then turned to those who were trying to hide cowardice
behind a mask of anxiety about food supplies and difficult
roads. 'You have the brazen effrontery,' I said, 'to deny the
efficiency of your commander-in-chief, or else to tell him
how to do his job.' However, though it was strictly my
business, I told them that the Sequani, Leuci, and Lingones
would be supplying grain as the harvest was now ripe. As
for roads—well, they would soon be able to judge for themselves.

Next, there was this report of intended mutiny. It did not,
I pointed out, worry me in the least: experience showed
that all cases of mutiny could be traced either to unfortunate mismanagement or to criminal avarice; whereas
my own lifelong integrity was beyond question, and the
Helvetian campaign evidence of my luck in war.

I then informed the meeting that I proposed to carry out
at once a plan which I had intended to defer: we were
going to strike camp between 3 and 6 a.m. on the following day, and it would at once be clear whether honour
and duty, or cowardice, were the stronger. If no one else
followed I would start with the Tenth Legion as escort:
of their loyalty, at any rate, there was no doubt. The Tenth
was indeed my favourite legion: they were a fine body
of troops, and completely reliable.

The result of this lecture was surprising. The spirit of
all ranks was changed, and they were now tremendously
keen to carry on with the fighting. To begin with, the

Tenth Legion offered thanks through their company commanders for the high compliment they had received, and
said they were fully prepared for active service. The rest of
the legions, speaking by their battalion commanders and
senior centurions, were then at pains to justify themselves.
They protested that they had never wavered, let alone
panicked: they had all along realized that the conduct of
a campaign was the business of the commander-in-chief,
and not theirs. I accepted their word for it.

The next step was a reconnaissance of the route, and this
was carried out by Divitiacus whom I trusted more than
any other Gaul. He discovered that by making a detour of
just over fifty miles the army could move through open
country. We started, therefore, according to plan, soon
after three o'clock; and six days later, after marching con-
tinuously, I was informed by scouts that Ariovistus's force
lay about twenty-two miles distant.

Conference of Tertre de Plettig

ARIOVISTUS heard of our approach, and sent a deputation
to say that so far as he was concerned the suggested conference might now take place: the distance between us had
been shortened, and he felt he could now comply without
risk. The offer was not rejected: this formerly unwelcome
proposal coming now from the German himself suggested
that he was beginning to see reason; there was some hope
that once he appreciated the nature of our demands he
would recall the many favours conferred upon him by
myself and the Roman Government, and would abandon
his unyielding attitude.

It was arranged that the meeting should be held four days
later; but in the meantime there was a frequent interchange

of messengers, and Ariovistus asked me not to bring a single foot soldier; he was afraid of being treacherously surrounded. He suggested that each party should attend with only a cavalry escort: on no other condition would he come at all. I did not want the conference sabotaged; on the other hand I dared not trust myself to Gallic troopers. The best plan, therefore, seemed to be to take all their horses, and mount troops of the Tenth Legion; thus, if need arose, I should have a perfectly reliable bodyguard. While this order was being carried out one of the men rather wittily observed: 'He's as good as his word: he said he'd make the Tenth his bodyguard, and now he's knighting us!'

The rendezvous was an earthen knoll standing in a wide plain and almost equidistant from both camps. The mounted legionaries were posted 200 yards away, and Ariovistus's horsemen took up their position at the same distance. He requested that negotiations be conducted on horseback, and that each of us should be accompanied by only ten men. We reached the spot, and I began by detailing the favours which he owed to myself and to the Senate. The Senate had allowed him the style of King and Friend, and had sent him magnificent gifts: I pointed out that this was a very rare privilege, and usually a reward for distinguished personal services. He, of course, had been granted that honour by mere grace of the Senate and of myself as consul: he had no right of audience, and his petition had rested upon no sufficient grounds. I went on to remind him that there were long-standing and very good reasons for the close ties between Rome and the Aedui: they had been highly honoured in numerous senatorial decrees, and even before they sought the friendship of Rome they had been the dominant people in Gaul. Rome desired on principle that her allies and friends, so far from losing any part of their possessions, should continue to grow in status and dignity: it was intolerable that they should be robbed of what they had on becoming our friends. I ended by repeating the demands already made through my envoys: he was to refrain from hostilities against the Aedui and their allies; he was to restore their hostages; and, though it might be not feasible to send any of his Germans home, he must allow no more of them to cross the Rhine.

Ariovistus replied briefly to this ultimatum, though he had a good deal to say on the subject of his own virtues. He insisted that he had crossed the Rhine not on his own initiative, but at the urgent request of the Gauls. He had left his home and family with high hopes, and these had been amply fulfilled: his settlements had been conceded by the Gauls themselves; their hostages had been freely surrendered; and the tribute which he exacted was only that which all conquerors impose on the conquered according to the acknowledged rules of war. He had committed no aggression—just the opposite: the Gallic states had combined to attack him, and in a single battle he had inflicted a crushing defeat upon their armies. If they wished to have another try he was ready to fight it out once again; but if they wanted peace they were not likely to obtain it by refusing tribute about the payment of which there had been hitherto no demur. Roman patronage, he said, should be rather a token of respect and security than an onerous liability;

that, at any rate, had been his idea in seeking it. If Rome took upon herself to cancel the tribute and release his subjects from their allegiance, he would reject the friendship of Rome as gladly as he had solicited it.

Turning to the introduction of German hordes, he urged that this was a defensive, not an offensive, measure, and based his assurance on the fact that he came only because he was invited, and had acted thereafter not as an aggressor but merely in self-defence. After claiming that he had entered Gaul before the Romans, and that on no previous occasion had a Roman army left the boundaries of the Province, he demanded to know what I meant by invading his possessions. Rome, he said, had her own province of Gaul; this was his, and our intrusion upon his jurisdiction was as unwarranted as would be an invasion by himself of Roman territory.

Next he took me up on my statement that the Aedui had received from the Senate the title 'Brethren'. He said he was not such a simpleton as to overlook the fact that Rome, in her late war with the Allobroges, had received no assistance from the Aedui, and had in turn given them none in their recent clashes with himself and the Sequani. 'I cannot but suspect,' he added, 'that your pretended goodwill is a sham: your army is here simply to terrorize me.'

He then announced that unless I cleared out and withdrew my forces from that area he would regard me as no friend, but a public enemy; and he assured me that my death at his hands would make him a popular hero in certain high places at Rome—the emissaries of more than one influential personage had assured him of that fact. He finished by offering me a substantial bribe to withdraw, and undertook, in return for his free occupation of the country, to make himself responsible for the successful conduct of such military operations as I might from time to time direct: and all without the least exertion or risk on my part!

I spoke at considerable length in an endeavour to explain why we could not abandon our present course of action. It was incompatible with my own principles and Roman practice to desert our faithful allies; besides, I did not agree that Gaul was any more his property than ours. The Ar-verni and Ruteni had been subdued [121 B.C.] by Fabius Maximus, but Rome had pardoned them: she had not formed them into a province, and had imposed no tribute. If priority of time was to be the criterion, Roman sover-eignty in Gaul was well established. If the Senate's decision were the test, then, by rights, Gaul was free, as the ruling of the Senate had been that she should remain autono-mous. . . .

At that point it was reported that Ariovistus's cavalry were moving closer to the knoll, riding up to hurl stones and javelins at our men. I finished speaking, rejoined my escort, and ordered them on no account to return the fire. There was obviously no danger in picked legionaries en-gaging a mere posse of horsemen; but it seemed unwise to join action, drive them off, and then have it said that I had surrounded them after giving my word not to do so.

The rank and file got to hear of the German's insolent behaviour at this conference: how he had told us to clear right out of Gaul, how his cavalry had attacked ours and thereby put an end to negotiations. Their spirits, as a result, rose yet higher; and they were more enthusiastic than ever for battle.

Next day Ariovistus sent envoys with a proposal to re-sume negotiations. He suggested I might once again fix a date or, failing that, send a member of my staff to represent me. I decided that no good purpose would be served by a

35

conference, especially as on the previous day the Germans had got so far out of hand as to open fire on us. To send a staff officer would be risky in the extreme: it would simply be turning the man over to a crowd of savages. The best course appeared to be to send Valerius Procillus, son of Valerius Caburius, who had received Roman citizenship from Gaius Valerius Flaccus. He was a highly accomplished and extremely brave young man; his loyalty was beyond question; he could speak Gallic, which, after long practice, Ariovistus now spoke fluently; and there appeared no reason why he should come to any harm. He would be accompanied by Marcus Metius, who had at one time enjoyed the hospitality of Ariovistus.

Their instructions were to find out what the German had to say, and then report back to me. But when Ariovistus caught sight of them actually in his camp, he shouted at them in front of his troops: 'What are you up to? Spying?' They tried to speak, but he silenced them and had them clapped in irons.

Battle of Mülhausen

THAT same day he moved his camp and halted at the foot of a mountain ridge, and the day after that by-passed our position and pitched camp just over five miles farther on so as to cut the road along which our convoys would have to travel from Franche-Comté and Burgundy (ex Sequanis et Haeduis). On five successive days I paraded my own forces in battle formation outside the camp, so that if he wanted to attack there was nothing to stop him. However, he kept his main army confined to camp during the whole of that time, though there were daily cavalry skirmishes. The following will give some idea of German fighting methods. They had 6,000 horsemen, each of whom selected from the whole infantry force a single companion as his bodyguard. These latter were extremely swift-footed and absolutely fearless. They accompanied the cavalry in action, covered their retreat, concentrated in an emergency, stood guard round any trooper who was seriously wounded and fell from his horse; and their training had given them such speed, that in the event of an unusually prolonged advance or rapid withdrawal they could cling to the horses' manes and keep pace with them.

When it became evident that Ariovistus was remaining close, I decided to reopen our supply route. A convenient site was chosen about 600 yards beyond the German position, and we proceeded there in triple line. The first two lines were to remain under arms, the third to entrench a camp.

Ariovistus dispatched some 16,000 light-armed troops and all his cavalry to try and scare us and hold up the work. But I stuck to my plan: two lines were detailed to drive off the enemy, and the third to carry on with their job. In due course the defences were complete; two legions and some auxiliaries were stationed there, and I took back the remaining four legions to the larger camp.

Next day, as usual, the enemy was given a chance to fight: troops from both camps were marched out and drawn up in battle formation not far from our main position. It appeared, however, that he was making no move, so about noon they were recalled. Then, at long last, Ariovistus sent a detachment to storm the smaller camp: there was some bitter fighting which lasted till evening, and both sides suffered heavy casualties. The enemy force withdrew at sunset. I questioned some prisoners as to why Ariovistus had not tried for a decisive action: the answer was that according to German custom it was for the matrons to decide by lot and divination whether or not they should give battle; and the matrons had declared that Fate was against a German victory if they fought before the new moon.

The next day adequate garrisons were left in both camps and the auxiliaries stationed in front of the smaller one, in full view of the enemy. They were intended to make a

show, for the legions were somewhat below strength considering the numbers opposed to us. Troops under my own command advanced in triple line against the enemy's camp, and he had now perforce to come out. He disposed his forces at regular intervals by tribes—Harudes, Marcomanni, Tribocci, Vangiones, Nemetes, Seducii, and Suebi—and, to make flight useless, his line was completely surrounded with transport wagons. These vehicles were filled with women howling, gesticulating, and imploring their menfolk, as they emerged, not to deliver them into Roman slavery.

The command of individual legions was entrusted to the chief of staff and other general officers, so that every man would have someone of high rank as witness of his bravery. I directed the action from the right wing, as the enemy's left appeared the least steady. Immediately the signal was given our attack was so furious and the enemy's onrush so swift and sudden, that there was no time to hurl pikes. The latter were thrown aside: it was a hand-to-hand fight with swords. The Germans followed their usual tactics, and quickly formed close order to receive the charge. Many of our fellows were seen to leap at the mass formation, wrench away their shields, and strike from above.

The enemy's left broke and fled; but his right was pressing us hard by sheer weight of numbers. This was noticed by our cavalry commander, young Publius Crassus; and as his movement was less restricted than that of officers in the thick of the fight, he ordered up the third line to support our harassed troops, and thereby turned the tide of battle.

The entire enemy force took to its heels: indeed they never stopped until they reached the Rhine some fifteen miles away. There a mere handful of them relied on their own strength to swim across, or found boats and saved themselves that way. Among these latter was Ariovistus: he managed to commandeer a small vessel which was moored to the bank, and so escaped. But all the remainder were rounded up by our cavalry and slaughtered.

Ariovistus had two wives: one, a Sueban, who had accompanied him from home; the other a sister of the Norican king Voccio, who had sent her to be married in Gaul. Both ladies perished in the general flight. Of his two daughters, one was killed and the other taken prisoner.

As I was riding with the cavalry in pursuit I came across Procillus: his guards had joined the rout, and were dragging him along shackled with three chains. This chance meeting delighted me no less than the victory itself: here was a man, one of the most distinguished Gallic provincials, my personal friend and guest, snatched from the enemy and restored to me: if Fortune had destroyed him, she would have taken something from the joy and exultation of that day. He told me that on three occasions lots had been cast in his own presence to decide whether he should be burned alive at once or kept till another time, and only the lots had saved him. Metius was likewise discovered and brought back to me.

News of this battle penetrated beyond the Rhine, and the Suebi, who had reached the right bank, started to return home. The Rhineland tribes, however, observed their alarm and followed, slaying a fair number of them.

It was rather early in the season; but two extensive campaigns had been concluded in one summer, and I therefore withdrew the army to its winter quarters in Franche-Comté (*in Sequanos*), appointed Labienus to command there, and started out for Cisalpine Gaul to hold the assizes.

BOOK TWO

[57 B.C.]

Belgic Conspiracy: Operations on the Aisne

Dᴜʀɪɴɢ that winter in Cisalpine Gaul there were frequent rumours that the Belgae (who, as already explained, formed a third of all the Gallic peoples) were plotting against Rome and exchanging hostages. Dispatches from Labienus told the same story, and the causes of this conspiracy were given as follows: [ᴀ] The prospect of a Roman invasion, once the subjugation of Celtic Gaul was complete. [ʙ] The prompting of certain Gauls: some of them were anxious enough to be rid of the Germans, but disliked the idea of Roman troops wintering, and perhaps making their permanent quarters, in Gaul; while others looked for a new order simply from natural restlessness and instability. [ᴄ] Anxiety on the part of influential chieftains: the supreme authority in Gaul was usually exercised by those individuals who were able to hire mercenaries, and their ambition could not easily be realized under Roman administration.

These rumours and official letters were disturbing. I raised two new legions in Cisalpine Gaul, and in the early summer ordered them to the further province under a deputy commander, Quintus Pedius. When supplies of fodder became available I rejoined the army, and instructed the Senones and other Gallic neighbours of the Belgae to make inquiries and let us know what was afoot. Their reports were unanimous: mobilization was in full swing; and as it was clearly unwise to delay moving against them, I made arrangements for food supplies, struck camp, and reached the Belgic frontier about two weeks later.

Our arrival was unexpected, earlier indeed than any one had anticipated, and the Remi (the Belgic tribe nearest to Celtic Gaul) sent two of their most distinguished citizens, Iccius and Andebrogius, as envoys. Their message was that they placed themselves and all their possessions under the protection of Rome and at her absolute disposal: they had not joined the Belgic conspiracy, they were ready to give hostages, to carry out whatever instruction they received, to admit us to their towns, and to supply food and anything else we might require. The remainder of the Belgae, they said, were under arms, as were the German tribes on that side of the Rhine. Their fanaticism had reached such a point, that the Remi had been unable to prevent even the Suessiones taking part, despite the fact that these latter were their own near kinsfolk sharing a common legal and political system under the authority of a single overlord.

Replying to inquiries about the states under arms, their size and war potential, they gave the following information. The majority of the Belgae were of Germanic stock; they had crossed the Rhine at an early period, and, because the land was fertile, had settled there and driven out the aboriginal Gauls. A generation ago, when the Teutones and Cimbri overran Gaul, the Belgae were the only people who managed to hold them at bay, and on the strength of that achievement they enjoyed a certain authority, and regarded themselves as a great military power. As to numbers, the Remi claimed to have the fullest and most accurate information: their geographical position and ethnological status made them members of the Plenary Belgic Council, and they therefore knew what forces individual tribes had undertaken to provide for the campaign. The Bellovaci, they said, came first in valour, influence, and manpower. They could put 100,000 men into the field, and had promised 60,000 picked troops from that number, demanding in return the general direction of the war. The Suessiones were immediate neighbours of the Remi, and their extensive territory was highly productive. Within living memory they had a king, one Divitiacus, the most powerful man in Gaul, whose overlordship included a large part of that region as well as south-east Britain. Their present sovereign was Galba, upon whom the supreme command had devolved with unanimous approval because of his integrity and ability. These Suessiones had twelve towns; they had promised 50,000 troops, as had the Nervii, the remotest and reputedly most warlike of the Belgic tribes. The Atrebates had volunteered 15,000, the Ambiani 10,000, the Morini 25,000, the Menapii 7,000, the Caleti 10,000, the Veliocasses and Viromandui 10,000, the Atuatuci 19,000; and they estimated the so-called German group comprising the Condrusi, Eburones, Caerosi, and Paemani, at 40,000.

After addressing some words of formal courtesy to the Reman envoys, I directed the whole of their council to assemble at my headquarters and to bring the children of their leading men as hostages. These instructions were punctually carried out in every detail. Next I had an urgent talk with the Aeduan Divitiacus, and explained how important it was for our own security, and indeed for that of both parties, to split up the enemy divisions, and thereby avoid having to engage the whole of their enormous host at once. It could be done, if Aeduan forces devastated the country around Beauvais (*fines Bellovacorum*), and he was dismissed with orders to that effect.

The Remi brought word that the entire Belgic host had concentrated, and was not far off, moving in our direction. Their report was verified by reconnaissance; so we hurried across the Aisne, north-west of Rheims (*flumen Axonam quod est in extremis Remorum finibus*), and pitched camp. This camp was protected on one side by the river-bank which covered our rear; supply routes from Champagne (*ab Remis*) and elsewhere were secured, and guards were posted at the head of a bridge which crossed the river at that point. Six battalions under a lieutenant-general, Quintus Titurius Sabinus, were left on the opposite bank with orders to strengthen their position with a twelve-foot rampart and a trench about eighteen feet wide.

Some eight miles distant was the Reman stronghold of Mont-Beuvray (*Bibrax*). The Belgae halted, and at once launched a furious assault upon this place; the defenders just managed to hold out until nightfall put an end to the attack. The Reman Iccius was in command at Mont-Beuvray: a man of the highest rank and reputation among his people, he was one of the envoys who had come to negotiate peace. He now sent a message to say that unless help arrived he could hold out no longer. Shortly after midnight, therefore, I sent a detachment of Numidian and Cretan archers with some Balearic slingers to the relief of the town, guided by Iccius's messengers. The arrival of this force stiffened the defence and revived their fighting spirit. By the same token the enemy abandoned hope of taking the place; but they delayed for a short time in the neighbourhood, ravaging the countryside, burning every village and building within reach. Then the entire host came on and halted within less than two miles of our position. Smoke and the light of watchfires showed that their

encampment extended over a front of more than eight miles.

My first decision was to avoid an engagement because of the enemy's numbers and his great military reputation. There were, however, frequent cavalry skirmishes on the basis of which I took stock of the enemy's prowess and the courage of my own troops. It eventually became clear that our men were in no way inferior. The natural formation of the ground before the camp was well adapted, ideal in fact, for occupation by troops in line of battle. The hill on which the camp stood rose slightly above the level: its front extended just far enough to allow room for the line in battle formation, it fell away steeply at each end, and in front there was a gradual slope down to the plain. From either extremity of this height, and at right angles to its axis, a trench was drawn about 600 yards long with redoubts at each end; and artillery was stationed in these redoubts to prevent the enemy outflanking us by sheer weight of numbers once we were in line and engaged. That done, the two newly recruited legions were left in camp, to be used as reserves if need arose. The remaining six were formed up in line outside, and the enemy likewise brought out his forces and deployed them for battle. He waited, hoping that we would be first to cross a small marsh that lay between the two armies; and we, in turn, stood ready to catch him at a disadvantage if he took the initiative. Meanwhile a cavalry skirmish was fought between the opposing lines: it was going in our favour, but as neither side made a move to cross the marsh, I took the infantry back to camp. The Gauls then hurried forward to the Aisne, which, as already stated, lay to the rear of our camp. Their plan was to storm the position commanded by Sabinus and to cut the bridge; or, failing that, to pillage the farmlands of Champagne (*agros Remorum*), which were of considerable strategic importance to us, and to intercept our supplies.

On hearing this from Sabinus, I crossed the bridge with my entire cavalry corps, together with some light-armed Numidians, slingers, and archers, and advanced to meet them. A bitter engagement followed: we attacked as they struggled through the river, and they lost many killed. The others made a remarkably daring attempt to cross on the dead bodies, but were repulsed by our heavy fire. Some of them had managed to get over in the early stages, but were mopped up by the cavalry.

The enemy realized that their hope of crossing the river, like that of taking Mont-Beuvray, had been foiled. It was evident, too, that we were not coming out to fight on unfavourable ground. As provisions were beginning to run short they summoned a council of war and decided that the wisest course was for every one to return home. It was agreed they should reassemble to defend whatever territory the Romans might first invade, and that in any case it was better to fight in friendly country with the use of local food supplies. Among the reasons which influenced that decision was the news that Divitiacus and his Aeduans were approaching the Oise (*finibus Bellovacorum*), and the Bellovaci insisted upon going without further delay to help their own people.

Accordingly they left camp an hour or so before midnight with tremendous uproar and confusion, in no fixed order, and under no official command. They were all keen to get home as soon as possible, and their jostling for first place on the road gave the impression of a headlong flight. The movement was promptly reported by scouts; but the reason for their departure was not yet clear, and for fear of ambush the legions and cavalry were ordered to remain in camp. At dawn, however, our information was confirmed by reconnaissance, and the cavalry under two general officers, Quintus Pedius and Lucius Arunculeius Cotta, were sent to delay their rearguard, Labienus following up with three legions in support. These forces made contact with the rear of the fleeing column, pursued it for miles, and annihilated a large part of it. The fact was that the enemy rearguard, when overtaken, halted and stood firm to meet our attack; but those in front thought they were out of danger. They were without leaders, and there was nothing to stop them; consequently as soon as they heard the din they broke and fled in disorder, and our fellows were free to work havoc all day long until sunset, when they stopped and returned to camp according to instructions.

Submission of the Suessiones and Bellovaci

NEXT day, forestalling the enemy's recovery from this terrible rout, we reached the plateau of Chaudardes, lower down the Aisne (*in fines Suessionum qui proximi Remis erant*), and after a long march halted before the stronghold of Noyon (*Noviodunum*). The place was said to be undefended, and I therefore attempted to storm it immediately on arrival. That, however, proved impossible: true, it was held by a mere handful of men, but the ditch was too wide and the wall too high. We therefore pitched camp, and then set about constructing mantlets and making the usual preparations for a siege; but on the following night, before these operations were complete, a whole crowd of Suessionian fugitives flocked into the town.

The mantlets were now brought up, earth was shot in to fill the ditch, and siege-towers erected. Works on this scale had never been seen or heard of in Gaul, and we moved with incredible speed. The Suessiones were unnerved: they sent a deputation to negotiate surrender, and their request was granted at the intercession of the Remi. Hostages included their principal citizens as well as two of King Galba's own sons. All arms in the fortress were handed over, after which their surrender was accepted.

We advanced from there against the Bellovaci, who had gathered with all their belongings in the fortress of Bratuspantium. We were still five miles away when their elders came out and intimated by cries and outstretched arms that they threw themselves on our mercy and would offer no resistance. It was the same when we reached the town: women and children stood on the wall and begged with their usual gesticulations for peace. They were supported by

Divitiacus, who had disbanded his forces after the Belgic withdrawal and returned to headquarters. He explained that the Bellovaci had always enjoyed the goodwill and protection of the Aedui. Admittedly they had broken off friendly relations and had taken arms against Rome: but they had only done so after being told by their chieftains that we had enslaved the Aedui and were subjecting them to every form of indignity and humiliation. The guilty parties, however, realized the disastrous consequences of their policy and had fled to Britain. The Bellovaci, he said, had Aeduan support in asking to be treated with what he called my 'well-known forbearance and magnanimity'; for his people's prestige would be thereby enhanced throughout the Belgic tribes, upon whose military and financial assistance they relied whenever they became involved in war.

In deference to the Aedui, and Divitiacus in particular, I accepted the submission of the Bellovaci, and agreed to spare them. But since they were the most influential and most numerous of the Belgic tribes, they were required to surrender 600 hostages. These were delivered; all weapons in the town were collected; and we moved on to the neighbourhood of Amiens (*in fines Ambianorum*) close to the Nervian frontier.

Operations against the Nervii: Battle of the Sambre

INQUIRIES about the Nervii and their way of life revealed that they admitted no traders and imported no wine or other luxuries, regarding such commodities as effeminate and destructive of the warlike spirit. They were a fierce, extremely hardy race; they sternly denounced the rest of the Belgic tribes for abandoning their traditional valour by submitting to Rome, and swore that they themselves

51

would neither offer nor accept any conditions of peace.

We had been marching through their territory for three days when some prisoners revealed that the river Sambre was only ten miles from where we had halted. The Nervii, they said, had taken up a position on the far bank to await our arrival: they had with them the Atrebates and Viromandui, two neighbouring tribes whom they had persuaded to risk the outcome of this struggle, and they were also expecting reinforcements from the Atuatuci. That was the sum total of my information, and a reconnaissance party was sent out with some centurions to select the best site for our camp.

A considerable number of Belgic and other tribesmen had, after formal surrender, been accompanying us on the road. Some of them, as was later discovered from prisoners, had during the past three days carefully observed the order of our march: they made their way to the Nervian camp under cover of darkness and explained that each legion was separated from the next by a long transport column, so that when the first legion reached the camping site the others would still be some considerable distance behind. It would be a simple matter to attack this first legion while still in heavy marching order; and once it had been dealt with and its baggage plundered, the others would not dare to make a stand.

The plan outlined by these informers received additional weight from another circumstance. The Nervii had practically no cavalry: to this day, in fact, they have very little use for that arm, relying entirely on infantry. They had, nevertheless, long since evolved tactics to check marauding parties of foreign horsemen. Their method was to plash young trees and bend them over so as to form a thick horizontal mass of branches. This was intertwined with brambles and thorns, and presented an obstacle as good as a wall, being impossible to see through, let alone to pass. Now these devices would be a serious hindrance to our column, and the Nervii decided that the proposed plan should certainly be tried.

The site chosen for the Roman camp was on some rising ground which sloped evenly from its crest down to the Sambre. Beyond the river and immediately opposite rose a similar height, the lower slopes of which were clear for about 300 yards. The upper part was densely wooded; and here the enemy lay concealed, only a few cavalry pickets being visible along the open ground by the river. The water was about three feet deep.

I sent the cavalry ahead, and followed with the rest of my forces: but the order of march differed from that described to the Nervii. We were getting close to the enemy, and, as usual on such occasions, I was riding at the head of the column with six legions in light marching order, followed by all the transport, which was covered in turn by the two newly recruited legions bringing up the rear. Our cavalry, slingers, and archers crossed the Sambre and engaged the enemy's horse, who repeatedly fell back on their main body in the woods, only to come out again and renew the attack. Our troops would not risk a pursuit beyond the open ground.

Meanwhile the first six legions to arrive had marked out the camp and begun its entrenchment. The natives, already deployed for battle and in high spirits, remained hidden in the woods: they had agreed to launch their attack when the head of our transport column appeared. As soon as they caught sight of it, their whole force made a sudden rush and hurled themselves against the Roman cavalry, who were soon in hopeless confusion. They then came down to the river at incredible speed: it almost seemed, in fact, that they were on the edge of the wood and in the stream at one and the same moment. With the same astonishing rapidity they stormed up the opposite hill to attack the men working on the camp.

I had a dozen things to do all at once; and many of them, indeed, could not be done at all—there was no time, the enemy was almost upon us. There were, however, two saving factors in this crisis: first, training and experience—the troops had learned in previous battles to use their own judgment and initiative; second, all legionary commanders had been instructed to stay on the site with their men until the fortifications were complete; they grasped the situation and, without awaiting further orders from me, took appropriate action on their own responsibility.

After giving such orders as were absolutely essential I rode down to address the troops. Quite by chance I came first to the Tenth Legion, and in very few words urged them to remember their traditions, keep their heads, and meet the onset firmly. The enemy was now within range, and I gave them the signal to engage.

Time was so short, and the Gallic charge so rapid, that the troops had no opportunity to don their helmets and uncover their shields, let alone to fix their distinctive badges. As they came down from their work each man lost no time searching for his own unit but joined the first group he met, regardless of its standard. The formation of our line, too, was dictated by the immediate requirements of time and place rather than by tactical theory. The legions stood at various angles to meet separate attacks, and the view was obstructed by those dense hedge-works which have already been described. It was therefore impossible to determine exactly where to concentrate reserves, to anticipate the needs of any given part of the line, or to maintain a unity of command; and in these most difficult circumstances the tide of battle inevitably fluctuated.

Our left consisted of the Ninth and Tenth Legions. Opposed to them were the Atrebates, now completely exhausted with running and weakened by heavy casualties. Under a hail of pikes they quickly fell back from the high ground to the river, followed by the legions who caught them as they attempted to ford the stream and killed large numbers in a sword attack. Our men wasted no time in getting across: they advanced up a formidable slope on the other side, and, when the enemy prepared to make a stand, re-engaged and once more hurled them back.

In another sector, at an angle to the first, the Eleventh and Eighth had likewise engaged the Viromandui, had cleared them from the heights, and were in action on the river bank. The Twelfth and Seventh were stationed close together on the right, so that the front and left of our camp were by now almost completely exposed. The entire Nervian force in one solid mass under their supreme commander, Boduagnatus, made for this point: one section of them began an enveloping movement on the right flank of the legions while the rest made for the hill-top on which the camp was situated. At the same time our combined force of cavalry and light infantry, which had been routed in the initial stages of the attack, was retiring on the camp when it came face to face with the enemy and took to its heels in another direction. The camp-followers, also, had watched from the rear gate on the summit of the ridge and seen our victorious troops cross the river. They came out in search of plunder, but when they looked back and saw the enemy actually in the camp they fled headlong from the scene. Meanwhile a tremendous din arose from the non-combatants in charge of the transport, and they too began to scatter, panic-stricken, in all directions. Our cavalry included some Treveran units; their reputation as soldiers is unique among the Gauls, but they were demoralized by this turn of events. Seeing the Roman camp swarming with enemy troops, the legions hard pressed and virtually surrounded, the camp-followers, cavalry, slingers, Numidians, all scattered and fleeing in utter confusion, and our position apparently hopeless, they hurried home with news that the Romans had been decisively beaten and that their camp and equipment were in enemy hands.

After addressing the Tenth Legion I had ridden over to the opposite wing, and found the troops at that point already in action, and in serious difficulties. Units of the Twelfth were huddled together, and the men, in consequence, so closely packed that they had no freedom of movement. Every centurion of the fourth battalion was dead; its standard-bearer had also been killed, and the ensign itself lost. Nearly all centurions of other battalions were either killed or wounded, including the chief centurion Publius Sextius Baculus, the bravest of the brave; he had been several times gravely wounded, and could no longer stand. The men were obviously tiring: some in the rear ranks had even ceased fighting altogether, and were intent only on getting out of range.

In front the enemy maintained relentless pressure as they poured up the hill, and were gradually closing in on both flanks. It was an ugly situation, and no reserves were available. I had come without a shield, but seized one from a man in the rear ranks and rode out in front of the line. There, after calling on every centurion by name and shouting general encouragement to the troops, I ordered them to move forward and open their ranks so as to allow room for their sword arms. They were now in better spirits— there was some hope: every man was eager to show his worth under the eyes of the commander-in-chief, regardless of his personal danger, and the enemy's advance was to some extent slowed down. The Seventh also appeared hard pressed, and I ordered the battalion commanders to manœuvre into a single square with the Twelfth. The effect of this movement was that it enabled the troops to support one another: they no longer feared an attack from behind, and their resistance began to stiffen. Meanwhile the two legions which had been detailed to protect the transport column and formed our rearguard received news of the engagement. They quickened their pace, and soon appeared on the crest of the hill in full view of the enemy. Labienus, also, had gained the opposite ridge and captured the enemy's base. From that position he could see what was happening in our camp, and sent the Tenth Legion to support us. These men had witnessed the flight of our cavalry and non-combatants; and realizing the grave danger threatening the camp, the other legions, and their commander-in-chief, they came up with all possible speed.

Their approach was the turning point of the whole battle. Even the wounded leaned on their shields and began fighting once more. The non-combatants saw the enemy waver, and ran unarmed to meet the attack. As for the cavalry, they were anxious to wipe out the disgrace of a cowardly withdrawal, and strove hard to outdo the heroism of the legions at every point of the field.

The enemy's courage was sublime in face of overwhelming odds. As their front ranks fell, the ones behind fought from their bodies; and as they in turn were mown down and the corpses piled higher and higher, the survivors, as if from a hillock, kept up a steady fire with their own weapons, and returned the volleys of our pikes which they had stopped. One must admit that only men of superb courage would have dared to cross a wide river, climb its steep banks, and then hurl themselves on a seemingly impregnable position; their magnificent bravery alone had enabled them to make light of such obstacles.

The battle of the Sambre ended in the virtual extinction of the Nervii. Their older men with the women and children had been herded together for safety among the marshes and tidal creeks of the Scheldt; but on receiving news of the catastrophe they realized the impossibility of opposing or of escaping our victorious advance. With the unanimous consent of the survivors, therefore, a deputation was sent to offer me their surrender; and in describing the extent of the tragedy which had overtaken their people they stated that of a national council of 600, only three members were left, and a military force of 60,000 had been reduced to barely 500 men. Wishing to demonstrate my traditional clemency towards those who submitted in the hour of their humiliation, I took special care to guarantee their safety: they were confirmed in their territorial rights and left in occupation of their towns, while the surrounding tribes were warned that no violence of any description must be done to the Nervii either by them or by their dependent states.

Treachery and Defeat of the Atuatuci

THE Atuatuci were descendants of the Cimbri and Teutones. At the time of their march on Italy via the Roman
Province these invaders had left such cattle and goods as
they could not take with them on the left bank of the
Rhine. The settlement was guarded by 6,000 men who,
for many years after the annihilation of their countrymen,
were harassed by local tribes, alternately on the defensive
and retaliating. Agreement, however, was finally reached,
and with the establishment of peaceful conditions the newcomers had chosen this region as their home.

Now the Atuatuci, as we have seen, were approaching
in full strength to reinforce the Nervii; but hearing the
news, they made straight for home, abandoned their towns
and smaller outposts, and concentrated in a single fortress.
The natural defences of this place were remarkable: it was
surrounded with high, precipitous rocks, and could be
approached on one side only by a gradual slope less than
200 feet wide. It had also been strengthened with a lofty
double wall, on which the defenders were now stacking
heavy stones and sharpened beams. In the first days after
our arrival they made a number of sorties, and there were
some unimportant skirmishes; but they were soon hemmed
in by a rampart twelve feet high, five miles in circumference, and with redoubts at short intervals. Henceforward
they remained within their walls, and with the aid of mantlets we began the construction of a siege-terrace. Some
distance off they could see us erecting a siege-tower, and
at first stood on the walls yelling abuse and jeering at the
very idea of erecting that enormous contraption so far
away. The Gauls, of course, are notoriously contemptuous

of our stature, which is small in comparison with their own huge physique; and they were puzzled to know how those little men with their puny hands and feeble arms imagined they were going to lift a heavy tower on to the top of a wall. They were seriously alarmed, however, by the strange, uncanny spectacle of the thing in motion, approaching their own walls. A deputation was sent to ask for peace: they had come to the conclusion, their envoys said, that Roman armies must have the aid of Heaven to be able to move up these gigantic structures at this speed. To their offer of unconditional surrender they attached only one request: they had heard reports of my leniency, and begged that, in the event of my deciding to spare them, they might not be disarmed; otherwise they would be defenceless against their neighbours, nearly all of whom were hostile and envious of their courage. They insisted that any fate at the hands of Rome was preferable to being tortured to death by their own subjects.

My answer was that the tribe would be spared provided they surrendered before a battering-ram touched the walls: not that they had any claim to such generous treatment, but it was my practice to show mercy. There could, however, be no discussion of terms unless they first handed over their arms. I undertook to do for them what I had done in the case of the Nervii—forbid the neighbouring tribes to molest them, since they were now subjects of Rome. The envoys took back these conditions, and returned later to say that they had been accepted. The townspeople threw down stacks of arms, which not only filled the ditch, but reached almost as high as our terrace and the wall. About one-third of the total had, as a matter of fact, been deposited in secret dumps; but this was not discovered until later. The gates were opened, and for that day there was peace.

Towards evening I had all troops recalled from the town and the gates shut. This was to prevent the men making trouble for the inhabitants after dark; but the latter, as we subsequently learned, had laid their plans on the assumption that we should withdraw our sentries or, at any rate, relax our watch, once the formalities of surrender were complete. Some armed themselves from their hidden stores, the remainder with shields of bark, or wicker-work hastily covered with skins; and soon after midnight they came out and made a sudden attack on a point in our fortifications which appeared easy to scale. Instructions had already been issued against such an emergency: the alarm was quickly raised by flares, and troops were rushed up from the nearest redoubts. The enemy, as was to be expected, fought with grim determination. They were a brave lot, and in this last desperate bid courage was all they could rely upon. We had the advantage of position, being able to direct our fire from earthworks and siege-towers: about 4,000 of them were killed and the survivors driven back into the town. Next day the gates, being now undefended, were smashed in, and our troops made their entry: I had the entire population sold at auction in one lot, and the purchasers' returns showed a total of 53,000 souls.

About this time I heard from Publius Crassus who had been sent with a single legion to deal with some tribes on the Atlantic seaboard. He wrote that all these had submitted and were now under Roman rule. The pacification of Gaul, therefore, seemed complete, and reports of the several campaigns made a deep impression upon tribes beyond the Gallic frontier. The native states across the Rhine sent embassies promising hostages and obedience to whatever commands they might receive; but as I was on the point of leaving for Italy and Illyricum they were told to come back early in the following summer. I left as soon as the legions were settled in winter quarters along the Loire between Orleans and Angers and in the immediate neighbourhood of our recent operations (*in Carnutes, Andes, Turonos quaeque civitates propinquae iis locis erant ubi bellum gesserat*). The receipt of my dispatches in Rome was marked by the proclamation of a fifteen days' public thanksgiving, a unique honour at that date.

BOOK THREE

[56 B.C.]

Galba in the Alps

I MMEDIATELY before my departure I sent the Twelfth Legion and a detachment of cavalry under Servius Galba to Savoy and the Valais (*in Nantuates, Veragros, Sedunosque*). He was authorized, if necessary, to quarter his troops in that area for the winter. My purpose was to open up the Alpine trade route which was dangerous for travellers and subject to heavy tolls. Galba fought a number of successful engagements and captured many strong points with the result that he received deputations from various tribes, accepted their hostages, and concluded peace. He then decided to station two battalions in the Chablais (*in Nantuatibus*), but to pass the winter himself with the rest of the legion at the little town of Martigny (*Octodurus*), which lies in the upper Rhône valley (*in valle non magna adiecta planitie*), surrounded by towering peaks. Martigny was divided by a river into two parts, one of which was assigned to the natives; the other was reserved exclusively for Roman troops, and fortified with a rampart and ditch.

Several days passed, and Galba was expecting the arrival of some corn when he was suddenly informed by a reconnaissance party that the Gauls had abandoned their side of the village under cover of darkness, and the surrounding heights were occupied by an enormous host of tribesmen.

This sudden decision to renew hostilities and overwhelm the legion was due to a variety of causes. First, the natives were not impressed by the size of Galba's force: its strength had been reduced by two battalions, and a considerable number of men had been sent farther afield to obtain supplies. Second, there was the strategic advantage: they would charge downhill, directing their fire into the valley from above, and it seemed that their attack must, from the outset, prove irresistible. Again, they resented the removal of their children as 'hostages'—to them it was simple kidnapping. Finally, they were convinced that Rome was interested not so much in securing trade routes as in the permanent occupation of the Alpine peaks and their annexation to the neighbouring Province.

The news found Galba with his defences still incomplete. He had also failed to build up adequate stocks of food and other material, thinking that the enemy's formal submission and delivery of hostages removed all likelihood of an attack. He immediately summoned a council of war and solicited their views. The situation, which had developed so suddenly and without warning, was extremely grave: the heights were swarming with armed men, and communications were cut, thereby preventing the arrival of reinforcements or supplies. The position indeed looked hopeless, and several members of the council voiced the opinion that the best course was to abandon their heavy equipment, cut a way out, and make for safety along the road by which they had come. The majority, however, voted to reserve that plan as a last resort, and in the meantinme to await developments and defend their camp.

After a brief pause, which barely allowed time to complete troop dispositions and carry out other arrangements, the enemy at a given signal rushed down from all sides and hurled volleys of stones and javelins against the rampart. Our troops were fresh and fought back with great gallantry: they held a commanding position, their aim was accurate, and they were quick to fill any dangerous gap in the defences. But the odds were against them: when the enemy grew tired after prolonged fighting they withdrew from the line and were relieved by fresh troops. That was impossible for our fellows—there were too few of them. A man might be exhausted, but he could not fall out, and, though perhaps wounded, had to remain at his post without any respite.

At the end of more than six hours' continuous fighting the endurance of our troops began to fail, and their ammunition was running short. The enemy assault, on the other hand, was more furious than ever, and as the strength of the legion gradually ebbed, they began to fill up the ditch and tear down the palisade. Two men saved this extremely critical situation—Baculus, the chief centurion, who was so badly wounded on the Sambre, and Gaius Volusenus, a most efficient officer and a very brave man. Together they hurried to Galba and told him there was only one last hope, and that was to break through the enemy lines. Galba assembled his centurions and ordered them to pass on his instructions to their men without delay. They were to stop fighting for a while and take merely defensive action. When rested they would break out, and after that their safety would depend entirely on their own courage.

These instructions were carried out, and there was a sudden rush from all four gates, which allowed the enemy no time to realize what was happening or to close his ranks. The tables were turned: the tribesmen had fully expected to take the camp by storm, but they were now themselves surrounded and cut off. Of an attacking force known to have numbered more than 30,000, over one-third was killed; the remainder fled in panic and were even cleared from the mountain slopes.

The entire enemy force had thus been annihilated, and, having stripped the dead, the troops withdrew to the safety of their fortifications. After this engagement, however, Galba was taking no more chances: the circumstances were in fact very different from what he had envisaged on arrival, and he was seriously concerned over the lack of food supplies. Next day, therefore, he set fire to every building in the place, and started back at high speed for the Province. No enemy barred the route or delayed his march; he brought his legion safely through to Dauphiny (*in Nantuates, inde in Allobroges*), and there spent the winter.

Operations on the Atlantic Seaboard

THE success of these operations appeared to mark the final pacification of Gaul. I was anxious to learn more about the Illyrian province by direct contact with the natives, and had started out early that winter when the Gallic war once again and quite unexpectedly flared up. The *casus belli* was the action of young Crassus who commanded the Seventh Legion in their winter quarters in Anjou (*in Andibus*). Food was scarce in that region, and he sent a number of junior officers and auxiliary commanders to arrange for supplies in Normandy and Brittany (*in finitimas civitates*). Among these agents, Titus Terrasidius went to the Esuvii, Marcus Trebius Gallus to the Coriosolites, Quintus Velanius and

Titus Silius to the Veneti. This last-named people were by far the most powerful on the coast of Brittany: they had a large fleet plying between their own ports and Britain; they knew more about the handling of ships and the science of navigation than any one else thereabouts; and their control of the few scattered harbours, which afford refuge from those violent storms so characteristic of the open sea, enabled them to levy tolls on nearly all who used those waters.

It was the Veneti who took the initiative by detaining Silius and Velanius, hoping thereby to recover the hostages they had surrendered to Crassus. Their neighbours—so impetuous is the Gallic temperament—were roused by this example, and with the same purpose in mind they arrested Terrasidius and Trebius. Envoys hurried from state to state, and their leaders pledged themselves to act only by mutual consent and to stand or fall together as the case might be. They called on the remaining tribes to guard their ancient liberties and not submit to the tyranny of Rome. The whole seaboard was quickly won over, and a joint delegation was sent to inform Crassus that if he wished to recover his officers he must restore the hostages.

I was a long way on my journey when this news arrived; but pending my return I sent orders for the construction of warships on the Loire, the drafting of rowers from Transalpine Gaul, and the enlistment of seamen and pilots. These preliminaries were soon under way, and immediately the season allowed I set out to rejoin the troops. The Veneti and other members of the league were informed of my arrival: they realized the gravity of their offence, and began to prepare for war on a scale proportionate to the danger confronting them. Their naval preparations were especially thorough, but they also relied to a great extent upon the geographical advantages of their country. They knew the roadways were intersected by tidal creeks, and could count upon our being hampered at sea by ignorance of the coast as well as by the scarcity of harbours. They were quite certain, also, that lack of corn would prevent our armies remaining in the area for any length of time. Even supposing all their calculations proved wrong, they were still masters of the sea: the Romans had no navy, no knowledge of the shoals, harbours, or islands in the theatre of war; and though the navigation of a land-locked sea might be easy enough, it was a very different matter to handle a ship in the vast open waters of the Atlantic.

Having chosen war, the Veneti set about converting their towns into fortresses and stocking them with newly harvested corn; a powerful fleet was also concentrated in home waters where it was assumed the campaign would begin.

I felt obliged for several reasons to undertake this campaign, notwithstanding the difficulties involved. The arrest of Roman knights was an outrageous insult; after making their submission and delivering hostages these tribes had resorted to large-scale conspiracy, open revolt, and renewal of hostilities; and, above all, if the league were not suppressed there was danger that other states would imagine themselves at liberty to follow suit. All men cling naturally to freedom, all men hate servitude; and bearing in mind the political instability of most Gallic peoples and their readiness to take up arms, it seemed advisable to make a more widespread distribution of forces before the league won further adherents.

A cavalry division started for the Rhineland under Labienus, who was to make his headquarters among the Treveri, but to maintain contact with the Remi and other Belgic tribes so as to ensure their loyalty. The Belgae were also reported to have summoned help from beyond the

Rhine, and Labienus had orders to prevent any attempt by German ships to force the passage of the river. Crassus proceeded to Aquitania with twelve battalions drawn from various legions and a strong force of cavalry: his duty was to see that no Aquitanian reinforcements were sent to Gaul, and thereby to prevent a coalition of two large tribal groups. Three legions under Sabinus were sent to isolate the Cherbourg Peninsula and Normandy (*Venellos, Coriosolites, Lexoviosque*), while young Decimus Brutus was entrusted with the command of our fleet, together with a Gallic squadron conscripted in Poitou, Périgord (*ex Pictonibus et Santonis*), and other subject areas. He was instructed to sail at the earliest possible moment for the south coast of Brittany (*in Venetos*). This was also the destination of our main land force which now began its journey under my personal command.

Most Venetian towns are built at the far end of long narrow headlands. The high tides which occur regularly every twelve hours prevented access by land, and approach by sea was no less hazardous because there was danger of our ships running aground at ebb tide. Direct attack was therefore extremely difficult. Resistance was overcome in some instances by enormous siege-works consisting of moles which held back the sea and brought us on a level with the town walls. Their naval resources, however, were immense: as soon as a position became untenable they concentrated a whole fleet of ships, evacuated the place, and withdrew to neighbouring strongholds where the defences were no less impregnable. Again, they had the benefit of foul weather during most of that summer: our ships could not put to sea, and the strong tides, together with an almost total lack of harbours, made sailing dangerous in that endless waste of waters.

The natives were not so handicapped, as will appear from the following description of their ships and rigging. These vessels were relatively flat-bottomed, and could therefore ride in the shallows or on an ebb tide. With their unusually tall prows and sterns they could weather high seas in a gale of wind; and the hulls, made entirely of oak, were capable of standing up to any amount of rough handling. The cross timbers consisted of beams a foot thick, fastened with iron bolts as thick as a man's thumb, and iron chains instead of ropes were used to secure the anchors. Their sails were made of raw hides or thinly dressed leather, due possibly to the absence of flax and ignorance of its uses, but more probably to a mistaken belief that canvas was unequal to the violence of the Atlantic gales and unsuitable for manœuvring vessels of that burden. In an encounter with these ships our sole advantage was speed derived from the use of oars: in other respects they were far better adapted to the conditions prevailing on that coast. Their bulk rendered them safe against ramming, while their height placed them virtually beyond the reach of our missiles and grappling-irons. Besides, when it began to blow hard and they were running before the wind, they were not only more seaworthy, but could heave-to in shallow water without fear of damage from reefs and jagged rocks; whereas all these factors constituted a serious danger to our shipping.

A number of strongholds had already fallen before I realized that so much effort was wasted: the loss of these places did not prevent the enemy's escape, nor were we in a position to do them any considerable damage. I therefore decided to await the arrival of the fleet. As soon as it appeared on the horizon some 220 enemy vessels dashed out of harbour and proceeded to their battle stations, magnificently equipped and cleared for action. Neither Brutus, our admiral, nor the officers and centurions commanding individual ships had the vaguest idea what to do next. They knew that ramming was useless, and even after the erection of turrets they were still overtopped by the high poops of the Gallic ships. It was impossible to discharge their weapons with any effect from this lower level, which merely added force to the volleys of enemy missiles. However, our men had prepared one device that proved most useful—sharp-pointed hooks fixed into the ends of long poles, not unlike siege-hooks in appearance. These instruments gripped the halyards, which were drawn taut and then snapped by rowing hard ahead. As soon as the halyards were cut, the yardarms naturally collapsed: and since the Gallic ships relied exclusively upon their rigging, once this was gone they came to an immediate standstill.

It was now only a question of courage and military skill, and our troops, aware that no instance of outstanding gallantry could pass unnoticed, soon carried all before them. They were fighting under the eyes of their commander-in-chief and in sight of the whole land army, which occupied the cliffs and every height affording a near view of the sea. As the yardarms of each enemy vessel collapsed, two or three of our own would haul alongside, and the troops storm aboard her. After the loss of several ships the natives realized what was happening; but there was apparently no way to oppose our tactics, and they determined on flight as the only solution. The ships, however, were already headed down wind when they were suddenly immobilized by an absolutely dead calm. It was exactly what we needed to complete our victory: they were overtaken and boarded one by one, and at nightfall, after an action

73

lasting from 10 a.m. until sunset, very few of them had managed to reach the shore.

This battle marked the end of hostilities against the Veneti and other coastal tribes: every tribesman capable of bearing arms had been called up to serve in the armed forces, regardless of age, rank, or experience; every ship in their navy had been recalled for operational duties in home waters; and all was lost. The survivors had no place of

refuge, no means of defending their strongholds, and they offered to surrender unconditionally. I determined to exercise the utmost severity as a warning to foreigners that the rules of international law affecting the rights of envoys must be properly observed: their entire national council suffered the death penalty, and the rest were sold into slavery.

While this campaign was in progress Sabinus and his troops entered the Cotentin, where the Venellian leader, a man named Viridovix, commanded a large army recruited by himself from the rebel states. A few days earlier he had been joined by the Aulerci, Eburovices, and Lexovii, who had closed their gates after massacring their legislative council for its refusal to endorse a policy of war. He had also been reinforced by a crowd of desperadoes and brigands to whom the prospect of loot and the love of fighting made a stronger appeal than the monotonous labour of farm-work.

Now Viridovix had encamped rather less than two miles from the Roman position, and led out his forces every day to offer battle. Sabinus, however, would not move, until at last the enemy began to regard him as a coward, and even ventured close up to the rampart. There was, indeed, some criticism on the part of his own troops, but he argued that no subordinate officer, especially in the absence of his commander-in-chief, should engage so powerful an enemy force without the advantage of position or other exceptionally favourable circumstances.

At this juncture, when his cowardice appeared beyond question, he chose one of his Gaulish auxiliaries, a man whose cunning was well suited to such a task, and induced him by the promise of substantial rewards to go over to the enemy. Briefed by Sabinus, he made his way to their lines, and, posing as a deserter, gave them the following information: The Romans were thoroughly alarmed; the Venetian campaign had involved their supreme commander in serious difficulties; Sabinus was taking his own troops to reinforce him, and intended to leave camp secretly not later than the following night. At this news they all clamoured for an immediate attack on the Roman camp—here was the chance of a lifetime, and it must not be missed. Their decision was influenced by several factors: Sabinus's hesitation during the past few days; the deserter's emphatic assurance; the inadequate steps taken by the Romans to meet their own food shortage; encouraging news from the Venetian theatre; and that common tendency of all mankind to wishful thinking. So obsessed were they by these considerations, that they would not allow Viridovix and his officers

75

to leave the assembly until they had agreed to their arming and marching without delay on the Roman position. The plan was approved; and, wild with joy as though celebrating a victory already won, they began their march on the camp, carrying faggots and brushwood to fill up the trench.

The camp was ideally situated on some high ground, at the top of a gentle rise about one mile long. The enemy rushed up this slope so as to allow their opponents the minimum of time in which to reach their stations and to arm. When they gained their objective they were out of breath, and Sabinus, after addressing his troops, gave them the signal they had so eagerly awaited: the Gauls were still loaded with their bundles when he ordered a sudden charge from two of the gates. Owing to the splendid position of the camp, their own exhausted state and inexperience, and the courage of our battle-trained men, the natives turned tail and fled without meeting even the first shock of this attack. They had no chance, and our troops, who were still quite fresh, pursued and overtook them: many were killed, and the survivors were rounded up by the cavalry—all but a mere handful who managed to get clean away. Sabinus heard news of the naval engagement at the same time as his victory was reported to me, and he received the submission of all the rebel states. For though the Gauls are ready enough to take up arms at a moment's notice, they are utterly devoid of that stern temper which survives defeat.

Crassus in Aquitania

ABOUT this time also Crassus arrived in Aquitania. He realized that extreme caution was necessary, for he would have to fight over country which had witnessed some years earlier the defeat and death of Lucius Valerius Praeconinus and the rout of the proconsul Lucius Manlius with the loss of all his equipment. He made arrangements for food supplies, recruited some cavalry and auxiliary troops, and called up a number of trained soldiers on the muster-rolls of Toulouse, Carcassonne, and Narbonne—three districts adjacent to the Gallic province. He then moved into territory inhabited by the Sotiates. Informed of his arrival, these people assembled a large army, and began operations with a cavalry attack on our marching column. They were driven off; but as our men followed up in some disorder an infantry force, which had lain in ambush in a valley, suddenly emerged and renewed the engagement. Some fierce and prolonged fighting ensued: the Sotiates were convinced, in the light of earlier successes, that the fate of Aquitania depended exclusively on their courage; while the Roman troops were eager to show what they could do under a young general in the absence of their supreme commander and without the support of other legions. The enemy, exhausted by heavy casualties, eventually broke and ran, leaving numerous dead upon the field. Crassus proceeded at once to the siege of their capital, and, as resistance was determined, he brought up mantlets and siege-towers. The Gauls attempted to interrupt these proceedings, first by direct attack, then by tunnelling in the direction of our terrace and its protective mantlets. They are brilliant sappers, for copper-mines and stone quarries are worked in many parts of

Aquitania; but the efficiency of our countermeasures demonstrated the futility of their efforts, and they sent a deputation to Crassus asking him to accept their surrender. He did so, and they handed over their arms in compliance with his order.

The attention of our troops was thus fully occupied when the tribal chieftain Adiatunus attempted a surprise attack from another side of the town at the head of 600 companions known locally as *soldurii*. According to the rules of their order, these men participate during life in all benefits enjoyed by their leader to whose companionship they have been formally admitted. In the event of his meeting a violent death, they fall together with him or else commit suicide; and there is no case on record of a man refusing to die with his leader.

Shouts from the corresponding sector of the Roman fortifications called the troops to arms. A sharp engagement followed, and Adiatunus was driven back into the town, where, in spite of his treacherous conduct, he prevailed upon the Roman commander to allow him the same terms of surrender.

When arms and hostages had been delivered Crassus moved into the Landes (*in fines Vocatium et Tarusatium*). The natives were terrified by the news that a stronghold well fortified by nature and by art had fallen within a few days of the enemy's arrival. Envoys passed between the tribes over a wide area, the league was cemented by an exchange of hostages, and general mobilization was ordered. They even sent to the border tribes of northern Spain for additional troops and military leaders, whose arrival made it possible to begin the war with very large forces and with absolute confidence. For the command was entrusted to officers of the highest reputation, who had served throughout the Spanish campaigns under Sertorius, and whose preparations followed the Roman model in the site and fortification of their camp as well as in the steps taken to cut our supply routes. Crassus was in no position to split up his small force, whereas the enemy could range over the countryside and block the roads without depriving their own camp of an adequate garrison. The consequent difficulty of ensuring the arrival of his convoys and the daily increase of the enemy numbers persuaded him that the issue must be determined at once by a decisive action. The matter was referred to a council of war: the members were unanimous in support of his opinion, and it was decided to fight the next day.

At dawn he led out his troops in full strength, disposed them in two lines, with auxiliaries in the centre, and awaited the enemy's next move. The Gauls regarded the outcome of a pitched battle as a foregone conclusion in view of their numerical superiority and their splendid military record; but they thought it better to play for safety and depend for a bloodless victory upon cutting our communications. Shortage of food, they argued, would inevitably compel the Roman army to retreat; it could then be attacked on the march, hampered as it would be in column of route with the men carrying their heavy packs. The Gallic commanders approved this plan, but although the Roman troops prepared for action, the enemy remained in camp. Crassus took in the situation: the restlessness of his own troops was increased by the enemy's inactivity which had all the symptoms of fright, and there were loud protests against further delay. He decided that the moment had come; he issued the customary order of the day, and, with the men's enthusiasm at its height, advanced to the assault. Some filled up the trenches, others drove the defenders from the rampart under a hail of missiles. Crassus had little confidence in his auxiliaries as fighting material; but they passed up ammunition, carried turf for the construction of a ramp, and thereby gave a convincing imitation of battle troops. The enemy put up a brave and determined resistance, directing their fire from above with considerable effect. In the meantime, however, a party of horsemen had made the circuit of their camp and reported that the defences on the far side were relatively weak and quite easy of access. Crassus asked his cavalry commanders to promise the men liberal rewards for their co-operation in a scheme which he then proceeded to outline. Certain battalions had been left to guard the Roman camp: they had taken no part in the engagement and were therefore still fresh. Led by these mounted guides they set out for the point indicated, and after making a long detour, so as not to be seen from the enemy's camp, reached their objective while attention was focused on the main action. They demolished the fortifications and gained a firm foothold in the place before the defenders were properly aware of their arrival or realized what was happening. The uproar in that direction was heard by the legions, and, as is always the case on the approach of victory, their strength revived and the fury of their assault redoubled.

The enemy, completely surrounded, fled to the ramparts, leaped down, and ran for their lives. But they were pursued by cavalry through perfectly flat country, and of 50,000 Aquitanian and Cantabrian troops known to have been present, barely one-quarter survived. The cavalry returned to camp very late that night.

On receiving news of this battle most of the Aquitanian tribes submitted to Crassus, and sent hostages of their own accord. They included the following:

Tarbelli, Bigerriones, Ptianii,
Vocates, Elusates, Gates, Ausci,
Garumni, Sibusates, Cocosates.

A few of the more distant tribes, relying for security on the
approach of winter, ignored their example.

Abortive Operations against the Morini

IN the general pacification of Gaul the Morini and Menapii
had remained in arms and sent no representatives to discuss
terms of peace. Wherefore, at about this time, although the
summer was far advanced, I marched against them, assum-
ing the campaign would be brief. Their tactics, however,
were entirely different from those adopted by the rest of
the Gauls: having witnessed the overwhelming defeat of
the most powerful states in the open field, they withdrew
into a part of their territory encircled by a ring of forest and
marshland. We reached the outskirts of this belt, and began
the entrenchment of a camp without catching a glimpse
of the enemy; then, as the men were working in scattered
groups, the natives suddenly rushed out along the whole
line of forest and attacked. The troops hurriedly seized their
arms and drove them back with heavy casualties; but they
ventured too far over this difficult ground and suffered
minor losses.

The succeeding days were spent felling trees, and, to
forestall a surprise attack while the troops were unarmed,
the timber was stacked parallel to the enemy's front and on
either flank. Working at incredible speed we cleared a large
area in a matter of days. The Gauls were moving deeper
into the forest; but their cattle and the tail-end of their
transport were already in our hands when the weather

deteriorated to such an extent that work had to be abandoned, continuous rain making it impossible to keep the men longer under canvas. And so, after ravaging the whole countryside and burning every village and farmhouse, the troops were withdrawn and quartered for the winter in Normandy (*in Aulercis Lexoviisque*) and other districts that had been recently in arms.

The story of the Gallic Wars, as told by Caesar himself, is one of the greatest classics of military literature. This brilliant translation by John Warrington brings it to life as never before. Instead of the awkward Latin syntax so many have struggled with in school, here is Caesar's living, breathing account of his triumphant campaigns as if he were telling them to us in English. Here is a Caesar few of us have ever known — intense, fascinating, and unexpectedly readable.

Caesar's account is as gripping as any of modern warfare. Filled with extraordinary tactical and strategic insights, *The Gallic Wars* seems contemporary. There are hostages, secret agents, mobilization plans, supply problems and the exchange of prisoners. It makes very compelling reading.

To the uninitiated, however, it might seem that illiterate tribes would stand little chance against the legendary legions of Rome. In fact, the Romans enjoyed no real superiority in arms or equipment. And the Northern Europeans were almost certainly better horsemen. What's more, Caesar had taken on one of the most testing of all military challenges: fighting an aggressive action on the enemy's ground, far from home.

Caesar triumphed by brilliantly outmaneuvering his adversaries. Using the superior Roman military discipline and engineering skills to every advantage, he attacked and defeated each independent tribe separately. By the time (52 B.C.) several tribes allied themselves to attack the Roman forces, it was too late.

Caesar's victory brought a vast extension of Rome's enlightened influences, and ultimately enabled him to seize power in Rome. By replacing the corrupt rule of the Roman nobility with an effective government, he prolonged the civilizing forces of the Roman Empire for nearly six centuries more.

The Gallic Wars by Julius Caesar is an essential addition to your *Leather-Bound Library of Military History*. The handsome volume is fully bound in genuine leather with a beautiful original design stamped into the cover. The hubbed spine is radiantly accented in genuine 22kt gold, the pages are attractively gilded, and the endpapers are of luxurious moire. It will be a noteworthy addition to even the finest private library.

Alexander S. Cochran, Jr.
Washington, D.C.
September 21, 1987

This collector's note was written by Dr. Cochran,
a professional military historian and author, expressly for
The Easton Press *Leather-Bound Library of Military History*
edition of *The Gallic Wars*.

The Easton Press

The Leather-Bound Library of
MILITARY HISTORY

Collector's Notes

The Gallic Wars
by Julius Caesar
Modern translation by John Warrington

Julius Caesar's invasion of Ancient Gaul (France) in 58 B.C. began one of the most pivotal military campaigns in history. Not only did Caesar's own future hang in the balance, but much of the world's as well. Defeat at the hands of Gaul's barbarian tribes would have hastened the end of Rome's power. Instead, victory prolonged the vast Roman civilization another 400 to 600 years. Had Caesar not triumphed in Gaul, today's world — with Rome's indelible imprint in language, art and politics — would surely not exist as we know it.

When Caesar began the eight-year-long Gallic Wars, Rome communicated with its holdings in Spain along the narrow strip of the French Mediterranean coast under its control. The rest of France, as well as the countries to the North, were in the hands of a variety of primitive warring tribes.

Although barbarian Gaul posed only a long term threat to Rome, Caesar saw it as an immediate opportunity. Not yet 45, and already a charismatic politician acclaimed for his oratorical brilliance, Caesar's ambition was limitless. His ultimate goal was the overthrow of the closely-knit nobility which ruled Rome. In his quite accurate view, their decadence was allowing Roman civilization to rapidly decay.

But in order to gain power, Caesar needed the aura of triumph — as well as the loyal manpower and money — that only military victory could bring. Almost as soon as he was named governor of the Roman portion of Gaul, he attacked beyond Rome's frontier.

BOOK FOUR

[55 B.C.]

German Invasion of Gaul

I N the new year Pompey and Marcus Crassus entered
upon their consulship; and during that winter two German tribes, the Usipetes and Tencteri, crossed the Rhine
not far from its mouth. Long provocation by the Suebi had
developed into open hostilities, farming had been brought
to a standstill, and wholesale migration was the result.

The Suebi are by far the largest of the German peoples:
they are said to possess one hundred cantons, each of which
provides an annual quota of 1,000 soldiers for foreign
service. The remaining civilian population supports the
army as well as itself, and next year relieves the troops who
then take their turn of home duties. Thus stock-rearing is
carried on without interruption side by side with military
instruction and field-training. There is, however, no private
property in land, and a year is the legal limit of residence
in any one place. The Suebi eat little cereal food: they
subsist chiefly on milk and meat, and spend a good deal
of their time hunting. From childhood they enjoy perfect
freedom of action without any kind of restraint or discipline; and that, together with their diet and constant physi-

cal exercise, makes them strong and of enormous bodily stature. Despite a bitterly cold climate they are used to bathing in the rivers and to wearing only skins, which are so scanty as to leave a large part of the body naked. They admit traders, but are concerned rather with finding an export market for the spoils of war than with any need of foreign imports. It is particularly remarkable that, unlike the Gauls who are extremely fond of horses and pay high prices for them, the Germans import none: their home breed, though small and ugly, is capable of the hardest work as a result of constant exercise. In cavalry actions these natives often dismount and fight on foot; but their horses are trained to stand quite still and can be easily remounted at a moment's notice. Moreover they consider it an indication of the most disgraceful effeminacy to use a saddle, and will engage the largest force of cavalry so mounted irrespective of their own numbers.

Imports of wine are absolutely forbidden on the grounds that it makes men soft and unequal to hard work.

As a nation they pride themselves on keeping the widest possible belt of no man's land along their frontiers, regarding it as evidence of the respect entertained by so many people for their military organization. It is said, for example, that on one side of the Suebic territory the country is uninhabited for a distance of about ninety miles. On another side their nearest neighbours are the Ubii who were at one time, by German standards, a large and prosperous people. They are slightly more civilized than other German tribes because they live on the Rhine, and frequent intercourse with merchants from nearby Gaul has led to their adopting Gallic customs. The numerical strength and determination of the Ubii successfully withstood repeated attempts by the Suebi to dispossess them. They were nevertheless reduced to the state of tributaries with considerable loss of power and prestige.

The Usipetes and Tencteri were in the same position. They resisted Suebic pressure for many years, but were eventually driven from their homes, and after wandering for three years in many parts of Germany, entered the Rhineland country of the Menapii who had land, farmhouses, and villages on both banks of the river.

Alarmed by the approach of this horde, the Menapii abandoned their dwelling on the right bank, and stationed pickets on the opposite side to guard the passage. The Germans tried every possible means to get over, but in vain: having no boats they were unable to cross by force, and to do so by stealth was impossible in face of Menapian outposts. They therefore pretended to set out for home, and the Menapii, informed by their patrols of the enemy's withdrawal, promptly reoccupied their villages on the German bank. After a three days' march, however, the invaders began to retrace their steps. Their cavalry indeed covered the entire distance in a single night: they took the unsuspecting Menapii by surprise, cut them to pieces, seized their boats, crossed the river before their countrymen on the opposite bank knew what was happening, took possession of all their farms, and lived on their food stocks for the remainder of that winter.

The receipt of this news aroused my misgivings as to its possible effect upon the Gauls. Their plans follow an ever varying pattern of emotionalism, they generally welcome political change; and it seemed unwise to rely upon them in any way. They have a remarkable habit of stopping every traveller, willing or not, and asking him what he knows, whether by hearsay or upon reliable evidence, about any topic that happens to interest them. In the towns a crowd will gather round foreign merchants demanding to know where they come from and what information they have from there. Upon such idle gossip they frequently base decisions of vital importance, which they quickly and inevitably regret; for whilst they themselves are slaves of mere rumour, their informants more often than not invent the answers most likely to please them.

I was aware of this habit, and to avoid becoming involved in what might prove a disastrous conflict I started earlier than usual to rejoin the army. On arrival I found my suspicions confirmed: some of the Gallic tribes had sent delegations to the Germans, inviting them to move southward from the Rhineland districts, and undertaking to supply all their requirements. Lured by this encouraging reception the Germans had continued their journey into the Meuse valley and Condroz (*in fines Eburonum et Condrusorum*), two districts controlled by the Treveri. The Gallic chieftains were summoned to my headquarters, but were given no definite information: they received instead a reassuring address calculated to allay their anxiety. Then after instructing them to furnish some contingents of cavalry, I announced my intention of undertaking a campaign against the Germans. I made arrangements for food supplies, enlisted cavalry, and started for the districts where the invaders were reported to be. Another three days' marching would have brought us to our destination when we were met by German envoys. I give the substance of their message:

The Germans, they said, were offering no challenge to Roman arms, but were ready to fight if provoked: it was their established custom to resist aggression from whatever quarter and with no attempt to bargain. There were certain points, however, that they wanted to make clear: [A] They

88

had not entered Gaul of their own choice, but because they had been driven from their homeland: and if Rome was disposed to accept their friendship, she might find them useful allies. [B] They sought a grant of lands or permission to retain what they had won by the sword. [C] They acknowledged the superiority of the Suebi (with whom, indeed, the gods themselves could not compare), but there was no one else on earth they could not conquer.

I replied in suitable terms, which amounted to this: No friendly relations could exist between us so long as they remained in Gaul. Failure to protect one's own territory did not warrant the seizure of other people's: besides, there was no land available in Gaul that could justly be assigned to them, especially in view of their vast numbers. They might settle, if they wished, among the Ubii, whose envoys were then at my headquarters complaining of ill treatment at the hands of the Suebi and asking my assistance: I would order the Ubii to receive them.

The German delegation said they would refer my offer to the appropriate authority and come back in three days' time: meanwhile they asked me not to move my camp any nearer. Once again their request met with refusal, for I had information that a large part of their cavalry had been sent some days previously across the Meuse in search of food and plunder, and I suspected they were playing for time until this force returned.

We were about seven miles from the enemy's position when the German envoys kept their appointment: they met us on the road, and did their utmost to persuade me from advancing farther. On my refusal to agree, they asked me to send orders forbidding an attack by our advance guard. At the same time they asked leave to send a delegation to the Ubii, and stated that they would avail themselves of my offer subject to the Ubian council of chiefs giving sworn guarantees of their safety. They would require three days to complete these formalities. As far as I could see, all this was part of the same ruse—to gain another three days pending the return of that cavalry detachment —but I consented to limit that day's advance to three and a half miles, the distance to the nearest watering point. I also suggested that as many of them as possible should attend at my headquarters next day, when they would be given a formal hearing. Meanwhile instructions were sent to the officers commanding our advance guard which consisted of the whole cavalry corps. They were ordered not to engage, but, if themselves attacked, to hold out until I arrived with the main body. Our horse numbered 5,000, whereas the enemy counted no more than 800 in the absence of their foraging party beyond the Meuse. Nevertheless

directly they caught sight of the Roman cavalry they charged, and soon had them in disorder. Our men, aware that the German envoys had just left me after negotiating a day's truce, were taken completely by surprise; they did rally, but the Germans, following their usual tactics, dismounted, unhorsed a number of them by stabbing the animals in the belly, and put the remainder to flight in such panic that they never drew rein until they came in sight of the column. In this action we lost 74 killed, including one Piso, a very gallant Aquitanian. He was a man of good family whose grandfather had been ruler of his tribe with the style of 'Friend' conferred by the Senate. Piso went to the assistance of his brother, who had been cut off by some enemy horsemen: he managed to save him, but his own horse was wounded and he was thrown. He struck back as long as he could, but was eventually hemmed in, and fell mortally wounded. His brother had by then got well clear of the fight; but when he saw what had happened he galloped up, flung himself on the enemy, and was killed.

This engagement was due to the treachery of a perfidious enemy who had actually begun hostilities after suing for peace. The idea of granting audience to their representatives or of listening to any proposals was now out of the question. It would have been sheer madness, on the other hand, to wait until the Germans were reinforced by the return of their cavalry; and knowing the excitability of the Gauls, I realized that this one German success must have made a deep impression on them; they must be allowed no opportunity to concert their plans. Having reached this decision, I notified my staff that I was determined not to lose a single day before bringing the enemy to battle; and early next morning I had an extraordinary piece of luck. A large party of Germans, including all their leaders and older men, called at my headquarters. They were playing their usual game of treachery and deceit: for though the ostensible object of their visit was to clear themselves of connivance in yesterday's attack in violation of an agreement made at their own request, they intended at the same time to inveigle me into granting an extension of the truce. I was delighted to have these people in my power and ordered their arrest. I then marched the whole army out of camp, with the cavalry bringing up the rear as they seemed disheartened by their recent defeat. With the troops formed in three parallel columns we made a rapid march of eight miles and reached the German encampment before they understood our purpose. They were suddenly and completely demoralized by our unexpected arrival in the absence of their own leaders: they had no time to make plans or to arm themselves, and were at a loss to decide whether to come out and meet us, or to defend their camp, or simply to run for their lives. Their consternation was evident from their cries and frantic scurrying. Our troops, enraged by their treachery on the previous day, stormed into the camp, where some of the defenders had managed to snatch their arms and fought from the cover of their wagons and heavy equipment. Resistance, however, was short: the invaders had crossed into Gaul with all their families, and a crowd of women and children now fled in all directions. I sent cavalry to hunt them down, and when the Germans heard their screams in the rear, and saw the massacre of their wives and little ones, they flung away their arms, deserted their standards, and rushed from camp. On reaching the confluence of the Moselle and the Rhine they realized that all further escape was barred: many of them were slaughtered, while the rest flung themselves into the water and perished, overwhelmed by terror, exhaustion, and the strong current.

The enemy numbered 430,000, and we had anticipated a very costly campaign: yet we returned to camp without one fatal casualty and with very few wounded. The Germans whom we held under arrest were given leave to depart; but they were afraid of being tortured to death by the Gauls, whose countryside they had ravaged, and desired to remain with us. Their request was granted.

On the conclusion of this German war several factors convinced me that we ought to cross the Rhine. My principal motive was to show the Germans that a Roman army could and would advance beyond the river, threatening the safety of their homeland, and thereby to discourage them from coming over so readily into Gaul. Secondly, there was that cavalry division which the Usipetes and Tencteri had sent across the Meuse in search of food and plunder. They had taken no part in the recent battle; but after the rout of their fellow countrymen they had withdrawn into Germany, and made their way into the territory of the Sugambri with whom they had joined forces. I had sent messengers to the Sugambri demanding the surrender of these fugitives who had made war upon Rome as well as on the Gauls. Their answer was that Roman sovereignty ended at the Rhine, and they asked upon what grounds I claimed any dominion or authority beyond the river since I held that the Germans had no right to cross over into Gaul. There was a third consideration. The Ubii alone of the German tribes had sent me an embassy: they had entered into alliance with us, had given hostages, and were now earnestly soliciting my help to deliver them from Suebic pressure. They said that the defeat of Ariovistus and this latest victory had conferred such glory and prestige upon Roman arms, even among the most distant German states, that the mere evidence of our friendship would afford them adequate protection; and they undertook to provide us with a large fleet of transports.

Such, then, were my reasons for crossing the Rhine; but to do so in boats appeared too risky, and was certainly below the dignity of a Roman general. To build a bridge would be a difficult operation because of the river's width, depth, and rapid current. Nevertheless I came to the conclusion that the difficulty must be overcome or the whole idea of crossing abandoned. Construction was therefore begun on the following plan. Two piles, 18 inches thick, slightly pointed at the lower ends, and varying in length according to the river's depth, were fastened together 2 feet apart to form a truss. They were then lowered into the water from rafts, and driven firmly into the river-bed with pile-drivers. They were not set in the usual vertical position, but inclining in the direction of the current. Opposite to them and 40 feet downstream a similar truss was fixed, but this time leaning against the stream. The trusses were joined by a transom 2 feet wide, the ends of which fitted exactly into the spaces between the heads of the four piles. The two trusses were kept apart by iron 'dogs', which secured each pile to the end of the transom; and added strength was given by diagonal ties running from one pile to its opposite number on the same side. In this way the rigidity of the whole structure naturally increased in proportion to the current's force; additional piles were driven in obliquely on the downstream side to form a buttress supporting each truss and helping to take the weight of water. A series of these trusses and transoms was connected by timbers laid at right angles and floored with long poles overlaid in turn with bundles of sticks. Other piles were set vertically a little above the bridge so that if the natives attempted to destroy it by floating down tree trunks or boats, these fenders would lessen the shock and prevent damage to the bridge.

Ten days after the collection of timber began the work was finished and the army crossed over. A strong guard was posted at each end of the bridge, and we pushed on into Sugambrian territory. Meanwhile deputations arrived from a number of states asking for peace and friendship, to which I gladly agreed and told them to bring hostages. But the Sugambri had prepared for flight on the advice of the refugee Usipetes and Tencteri immediately the construction of our bridge was started: they evacuated their territory, removed all their belongings, and hid themselves in a dense forest region. After spending a few days in that district, burning all their villages and farm buildings and cutting down their crops, we moved on into Ubian territory where I promised assistance in the event of an open attack by the Suebi, and received the following report from the tribesmen. The Suebi, they said, had been informed by their patrols of our bridging operations. As usual in such an emergency, they had held a council and sent messengers to all districts ordering every one to leave their homes: women and children were to be concealed in the woods, together with all movable property, while those fit for military service mustered at a point almost exactly in the centre of their territory. There they were apparently awaiting our arrival, determined to fight a decisive action on the spot. That was my information. But the objects of our crossing had all been achieved: the Germans were overawed, the Sugambri punished, and the Ubii relieved of Suebic pressure. We had spent altogether eighteen days beyond the Rhine, and I felt that the demands of honour and interest had been satisfied. We therefore recrossed into Gaul, destroying the bridge behind us.

First British Expedition

SUMMER was now drawing to a close, and winter sets in rather early in these parts, as Gaul lies wholly in northern latitudes. Nevertheless I hurried on preparations for an expedition to Britain, knowing that Britain had rendered assistance to the enemy in nearly all my Gallic campaigns. Although it was too late in the year for military operations I thought it would be a great advantage merely to have visited the island, to have seen what kind of people the inhabitants were, and to have learned something about the country with its harbours and landing-places. Of all this the Gauls knew virtually nothing; for no one except traders makes the journey with any regularity, and even their knowledge is limited to the sea coast immediately facing Gaul. Interviews with numerous merchants elicited nothing as to the size of the island, the names and strength of the native tribes, their military and civil organization, or the harbours which might accommodate a large fleet. Nevertheless it seemed essential to obtain this information before risking an expedition, and Caius Volusenus appeared to me the best man for the job. He travelled in a warship with orders to make a general reconnaissance and report back as early as possible. Meanwhile the whole army moved into Artois (*in Morinos*), where the mainland is nearest to the coast of Britain; and ships were ordered to assemble there from all neighbouring districts, including the fleet which had been built last year for the Venetian campaign. Meanwhile, however, some traders revealed our plans to the Britons, and a number of tribes sent envoys promising hostages and offering their submission. They were received in audience, promised generous terms, and urged to abide by their undertaking. They were accompanied on their return journey by Commius, whom I had appointed ruler of the Atrebates after the subjugation of that people, and of whose honour, discretion, and loyalty I had received abundant proof. Commius was greatly respected in Britain, and his orders were to visit all the states he could, impressing on them the advantages of Roman protection, and to announce my impending arrival.

Volusenus completed his survey as far as he was able without disembarking and risking a hostile reception from the natives. Five days later he returned and made his report. While the ships were commissioning, delegations arrived from a large section of the Morini. They excused themselves for their recent hostile attitude on the grounds that they were uncivilized folk, ignorant of Roman institutions, but they promised obedience for the future. Their action was providential: for though I had no wish to leave an enemy hanging on my rear, the season was too far advanced to start another campaign; and in any case the British expedition was clearly more important than the conquest of these petty states. I therefore demanded a large number of hostages and, when they arrived, accepted the submission of the Morini.

A fleet of about eighty ships, which seemed adequate for the conveyance of two legions, was eventually commissioned and assembled, together with a number of warships commanded by the chief of staff, officers of general rank, and auxiliary commanders. At another port, some eight miles higher up the coast, were eighteen transports which had been prevented by adverse winds from joining the main fleet at Boulogne (*Portus Itius*): these were allotted to the cavalry. The remainder of the army under Sabinus and Cotta was sent on a punitive expedition against the Me-

napii and those cantons of the Morini which had not been
represented in the recent delegation. Another general officer, Publius Sulpicius Rufus, was ordered to guard the
harbour with a force that seemed large enough for that
purpose.

Arrangements were now complete, the weather was
favourable, and we cast off just before midnight. The
cavalry had been ordered to make for the northern port,
embark there, and follow on; but they were rather slow
about carrying out these instructions, and started, as we
shall see, too late. I reached Britain with the leading vessels
at about 9 a.m., and saw the enemy forces standing under
arms all along the heights. At this point of the coast precipitous cliffs tower over the water, making it possible to
fire from above directly on to the beaches. It was clearly
no place to attempt a landing, so we rode at anchor until
about 3.30 p.m. awaiting the rest of the fleet. During this
interval I summoned my staff and company commanders,
passed on to them the information obtained by Volusenus,
and explained my plans. They were warned that, as tactical
demands, particularly at sea, are always uncertain and subject to rapid change, they must be ready to act at a moment's notice on the briefest order from myself. The meeting then broke up: both wind and tide were favourable,
the signal was given to weigh anchor, and after moving
about eight miles up channel the ships were grounded on
an open and evenly shelving beach.

The natives, however, realized our intention: their cavalry and war chariots (a favourite arm of theirs) were sent
ahead, while the main body followed close behind and
stood ready to prevent our landing. In the circumstances,
disembarkation was an extraordinarily difficult business. On
account of their large draught the ships could not be

beached except in deep water. My troops, besides being ignorant of the locality, had their hands full: weighted with a mass of heavy armour, they had to jump from the ships, stand firm in the surf, and fight at the same time. But the enemy knew their ground: being quite unencumbered, they could hurl their weapons boldly from dry land or shallow water, and gallop their horses which are trained for this kind of work. Our men were terrified: they were new to these tactics, and lacked that dash and drive which had always characterized their land battles.

The warships, however, were of a shape unfamiliar to the natives; they were swift, too, and easier to handle than the transports. Therefore, as soon as I grasped the situation I ordered them to go slightly astern, clear of the transports, then full speed ahead, bringing up on the Britons' right flank. From that position they were to open fire and force the enemy back with slings, arrows, and artillery. The manœuvre was of considerable help to the troops. The Britons were scared by the strange forms of the warships, by the motion of the oars, and by the artillery which they had never seen before: they halted, then fell back a little; but our men still hesitated, mainly because of the deep water.

At this critical moment the standard-bearer of the Tenth Legion, after calling on the gods to bless the legion through his act, shouted: 'Come on, men! Jump, unless you want to betray your standard to the enemy! I, at any rate, shall do my duty to my country and my commander.' He threw himself into the sea and started forward with the eagle. The rest were not going to disgrace themselves; cheering wildly they leaped down, and when the men in the next ships saw them they too quickly followed their example.

The action was bitterly contested on both sides. But

our soldiers were unable to keep their ranks and stand firm. They failed to rejoin their own units: men from different ships fell in under the first standard they reached, and a good deal of confusion resulted. The Britons, of course, knew all the shallows: standing on dry land, they watched the men disembark in small parties, galloped down, attacked them as they struggled through the surf, and surrounded them with superior numbers while others opened fire on the exposed flank of isolated units. I therefore had the warships' boats and scouting vessels filled with troops, so that help could be sent to any point where the men seemed to be in difficulties. When every one was ashore and formed up, the legions charged: the enemy was hurled back, but pursuit for any distance was impossible as the cavalry transports had been unable to hold their course and make the island. That was the only thing that deprived us of a decisive victory.

The natives eventually recovered from their panic and sent a delegation to ask for peace, promising to surrender hostages and carry out my instructions. These envoys brought with them Commius, who, it will be remembered, had preceded us to Britain. When he had landed and was actually delivering my message in the character of an ambassador he had been arrested and thrown into prison. Now, after their defeat, the natives sent him back: in asking for peace they laid the blame for this outrage upon the common people and asked me to overlook the incident on the grounds of their ignorance. I protested against this unprovoked attack which they had launched after sending a mission to the Continent to negotiate a friendly settlement, but agreed to pardon their ignorance and demanded hostages. Some of these were handed over at once, others, they said, would have to be fetched from a distance and would be delivered in a few days. Meanwhile they were ordered to return to their occupations on the land, and chieftains began to arrive from the surrounding districts, commending themselves and their tribes to my protection. Peace was thus concluded.

Late on the fourth day after our landing in Britain the eighteen transports with cavalry on board had sailed from the northern port with a gentle breeze; but as they neared the British coast and were within sight of the camp a violent storm had blown up, and none of them could hold their course. Some had been driven back to the point of embarkation; others, in great peril, had been swept down channel, westwards, towards the southernmost part of the island. Notwithstanding the danger, they  had dropped anchor, but now shipped so much water that they were obliged to stand out to sea as darkness fell and return to the Continent.

It happened to be full moon that night; and at such times the Atlantic tides are particularly high, a fact of which we were ignorant. The result was that the warships, which had been beached, became waterlogged: as for the transports riding at anchor, they were dashed one against another, and it was impossible to manœuvre them or to do anything whatever to assist. Several ships broke up, and the remainder lost their cables, anchors, and rigging. Consternation naturally seized the troops, for there were no spare ships in which they could return and no means of refitting.

It had been generally understood, too, that we should winter in Gaul, and consequently no arrangements had been made for food supplies in Britain.

The British chieftains at my headquarters sized up the situation and put their heads together. They knew we had no cavalry and were short of grain and shipping; they judged the weakness of our forces from the inconsiderable area of the camp, which was all the smaller because we had brought no heavy equipment; and they decided to renew the offensive. Their aim was to cut us off from food supplies and other material and to prolong the campaign until winter. They were confident that if the present expeditionary force were wiped out or prevented from returning, an invasion of Britain would never again be attempted. Accordingly they renewed their vows of mutual loyalty, slipped away one by one from our camp, and secretly reassembled their forces from the countryside.

I had not yet been informed of their intention; but, in view of the disaster to our shipping and the fact that they had ceased to deliver hostages, I had a suspicion of what might happen, and was prepared for any emergency. Corn was brought in every day from the fields; timber and bronze from the badly damaged vessels were used to repair others; the necessary equipment was ordered from the Continent; and, thanks to the energy and efficiency of the troops, all but twelve ships were made tolerably seaworthy.

One day while these repairs were in progress the Seventh Legion was doing its turn in the harvest field: nothing had occurred as yet to arouse suspicion of an impending attack, for many of the natives were still at work on the land and others were frequent visitors to our camp. Suddenly, however, the sentries on the gates reported an unusually large dust cloud in the direction in which the legion had gone.

My suspicions were confirmed—the natives had hatched some new plot.

The battalions on guard duty were detailed to go with me to the scene of action, two others were ordered to relieve them, and the rest to arm and follow on immediately. We had not been marching long before I noticed the Seventh was in difficulties: they were only just managing to hold their ground with their units closely packed and under heavy fire. The fact was, the enemy had guessed their destination, as the fields were already stripped elsewhere: they had hidden themselves in the woods by night, and attacked while the men were unarmed and busy reaping. We lost a few killed. The rest were in confusion before they could form up, and found themselves hemmed in by cavalry and war chariots.

The following will give some idea of British charioteers in action. They begin by driving all over the field, hurling javelins; and the terror inspired by the horses and the noise of the wheels is usually enough to throw the enemy ranks into disorder. Then they work their way between their own cavalry units, where the warriors jump down and fight on foot. Meanwhile the drivers retire a short distance from the fighting and station the cars in such a way that their masters, if outnumbered, have an easy means of retreat to their own lines. In action, therefore, they combine the mobility of mounted troops with the steadiness of infantry. Their skill, which is derived from ceaseless training and practice, may be judged by the fact that they can control their horses at full gallop on the steepest incline, check and turn them in a moment, run along the pole, stand on the yoke, and get back again into the chariot as quick as lightning.

Our troops were unnerved by these tactics, and help

reached them in the nick of time: for as we approached the enemy halted, and the legion recovered its morale. The moment, however, was clearly inopportune to precipitate a general engagement; so I advanced no farther, and shortly afterwards led the troops back to camp. This episode kept us all fully occupied, and such natives as were still at work in the fields made off.

There followed several days of bad weather, which confined us to camp besides preventing an enemy attack. But during this interval the Britons sent runners all over the countryside to inform the population that our force was very weak, and that if it could be driven from its base they had every chance of obtaining valuable loot and of securing their freedom once and for all. A strong British force of both arms was assembled and marched on our camp. It was fairly evident that what had happened before would happen again—even if we routed them, their speed would enable them to get clear of further danger. Nevertheless, there were now available some thirty horses brought over by Commius. So the legions were drawn up in battle formation in front of the camp, and after a brief action the enemy was overwhelmed and fled. We followed as far as our speed and endurance allowed, killed a large number of them, then burned all their dwellings over a wide area, and returned to base.

That same day envoys came to sue for peace: they were met with a demand for twice as many hostages as before, and were ordered to bring them over to the Continent, because the equinox was close at hand and the ill condition of our ships made it inadvisable to postpone the voyage until winter. Taking advantage of fair weather we set sail a little after midnight, and the whole fleet reached the mainland in safety.

Two transports, however, with about 300 troops on board failed to make the same port as the rest and were carried a little farther south. When these men disembarked and were on the march to their base they were surrounded by a small party of Morini and given the alternative of surrender or death. This tribe had been subdued before we left for Britain, but the temptation to plunder had proved too strong. The Romans formed a circle and defended themselves; but the din brought about 6,000 more natives on the scene. Immediately on hearing this news I sent the cavalry in full strength to their assistance; but in the meantime they stood their ground, putting up a magnificent fight for almost four hours and inflicting heavy casualties at the cost of only a few wounded. On the appearance of our horse the Morini threw away their arms and ran, leaving many dead on the field.

Next day Labienus was sent against the rebellious tribe with the legions that had just returned from Britain. The marshes which had offered some protection last year had now dried up: the enemy had no place of refuge left, and nearly all gave themselves up to the Roman commander.

Sabinus and Cotta on their expedition against the Menapii had been able to do no more than pillage the country, cutting down crops and burning houses; for the natives had concealed themselves in an area of thick forest. Both officers now returned to headquarters with their troops, and I arranged for all the legions to winter in Belgic territory. Only two British tribes sent over hostages: the rest ignored my instructions.

Upon receipt of my dispatches announcing these achievements the Senate decreed a twenty days' public thanksgiving.

BOOK FIVE

[54 B.C.]

Preparations for a Second British Expedition

I N the consulship of Lucius Domitius and Appius Clau-
dius, on the eve of my departure for Italy (a journey I
had been making annually for the past few years), I
directed my staff to arrange for the building of as many
ships as possible during the winter and to have the old ones
repaired. Detailed instructions were left for the dimensions
and shape of these new vessels. To simplify loading and
beaching they were to be constructed with a somewhat
lower freeboard than that commonly used in the Mediterranean, especially as I had noticed that, owing to the frequent ebb and flow of tides, the waves in the Channel are
comparatively small. To allow for heavy cargoes, including numerous pack-animals, they were to be rather wider
in the beam than those used in other waters; and all were
to be fitted with sails as well as oars, an arrangement which
was greatly facilitated by their low freeboard. Materials
for their equipment were ordered from Spain.

After concluding the assizes in northern Italy I started for
Illyricum because of reports that the Pirustae were raiding
over the adjacent frontier and causing serious damage in

that province. On arrival I ordered the native states to levy troops, and named a place for their assembly; the Pirustae, however, got news of this and sent representatives to say that none of the raids had the authority of their government, which was ready to make full reparation. I accepted their assurance and demanded hostages, but made it quite clear that unless they were handed over by a fixed date it would mean war.

The hostages were punctually delivered, and arbitrators were then appointed to assess the damage suffered by the various tribes and to decide what reparation was due.

After disposing of that business and holding assizes I returned to northern Italy and from there started back to rejoin the army. Soon after my arrival in Gaul I began a tour of the winter camps, and found that, notwithstanding grave shortage of materials, the troops had worked so hard that there were about 600 ships of the types described, including 18 transports, ready for launching in a few days. After congratulating the men and those in charge of the work, I gave instructions that all vessels were to assemble at Boulogne, which had been found by experience to be the most convenient starting-point for the Channel crossing, being some twenty-eight miles from the coast of Britain. Sufficient troops were left to carry out these orders while I started with four legions in light marching order and 800 cavalry for the Moselle basin (*in fines Treverorum*) where, according to reports, the Treveri were defying orders by absenting themselves from the annual Gallic diets and were making overtures to the Germans beyond the Rhine.

The Treveri, it will be remembered, are a Rhineland tribe: they have the most powerful cavalry corps in Gaul as well as strong forces of infantry, and two of their chieftains—Indutiomarus and Cingetorix—were at this time contending for supreme authority. Directly Cingetorix learned of our approach he paid me a visit, emphasized that he and his followers intended to support the Roman alliance, and gave me an account of the state of affairs in his country. Indutiomarus, on the other hand, began preparing for war: he assembled forces of cavalry and infantry, and concealed all those above or below military age in the great forest of Ardennes, which stretches from the Rhine through Treveran territory to the eastern borders of Champagne (*ad initium Remorum*). However, some of his most important followers, influenced by their personal friendship with Cingetorix, and frightened by the approach of a Roman army, came to meet me. They said there was nothing they could do to help their country, and made certain requests with an eye to their personal interests. Indutiomarus now feared complete isolation: he sent representatives who apologized on behalf of their chief for his failure to put in an appearance, and explained that his presence at home was necessary to ensure the loyalty of his subjects. If every man of rank, the message went on, were to make this journey, there was danger that the ignorant masses might be led astray. As it was, he had everything under control, and intended, subject to my approval, to visit me in camp, where he would place himself and his tribe under my protection.

The motive behind this statement was clear enough; it was obvious, too, what prevented him going ahead with his original design: but I did not want to have to spend the whole summer in that part of the world when arrangements for the British expedition were complete. I therefore ordered Indutiomarus to present himself with 200 hostages, naming in particular his son and all his near relatives. They arrived in due course, and I told him he had nothing to fear as long as he remained loyal. At the same time, how-

ever, I summoned other dignitaries of the tribe and won
them over individually to Cingetorix. He fully deserved
this expression of confidence; but there were also diplo-
matic reasons for strengthening the authority of a man of
such outstanding loyalty. Indutiomarus, however, was
mortally offended by the gesture, which struck at his own
power and fanned the flames of animosity which he already
felt towards Rome.

After settling that matter we made our way back to
Boulogne and found that 60 ships built on the lower Marne
(*in Meldis*) had been driven off their course by a storm, and
had returned to their starting point: the rest were in com-
mission and ready to sail. The entire Gallic cavalry corps
of 4,000 horse now assembled at the port, as well as the
most prominent citizens from every state. Being afraid of
a rising in Gaul during my absence, I had decided to leave
behind only a few of these men, whose loyalty was beyond
question, and to take the others as hostages.

Among these Gallic leaders was the notorious Dumnorix.
I was resolved from the start to keep him with me, for
I knew him to be at heart a revolutionary, ambitious,
brave, and highly respected by his fellow Gauls. Furthermore, he had stated in the Aeduan council that I had
offered to make him ruler of the tribe, a claim which the
Aedui strongly resented: they had not dared to send an open
rejection of, or even to protest against, such a proposal,
but I learned the truth from some friends at whose house
I had stayed. At all events, Dumnorix began by pressing for
leave to remain in Gaul: he said he was not used to sailing
and was frightened of the sea; also that religious obligations
made his presence at home absolutely essential. When he
realized I was adamant and there was no chance of getting
his own way, he approached the Gallic chiefs, talked with

them privately one by one, and urged them to remain on the Continent. He argued that I must have some ulterior motive in robbing Gaul of all her leading citizens: no doubt I shrank from putting them to death openly in their own country, and therefore meant to do so as soon as I got them over to Britain. He suggested that they should all bind themselves by oath to work together for a better Gaul.

The foregoing information was derived from various sources; and because of my very high regard for the Aedui I came to the conclusion that Dumnorix must at all costs be restrained and prevented from achieving his ends. Since his fanaticism was going from bad to worse, precautions were necessary to forestall an attempt on my own life and possible damage to Roman interests. We were detained at Boulogne for just over three weeks by the prevailing north-west winds, and in the meantime I did my best to hold Dumnorix to his allegiance while keeping myself informed of his every move. The bad weather eventually lifted: all troops were ordered to embark, and while this operation was proceeding Dumnorix left camp without my knowledge at the head of some Aeduan horse. He made straight for home: but directly his escape was reported I postponed the sailing date, laid aside all other business, and sent a strong cavalry detachment in pursuit.

Their orders were to bring him back alive unless he refused and offered resistance, in which case he was to be killed; for a man who flouted my authority to my face could clearly not be trusted to behave like a rational being behind my back. When called on to halt he resisted violently, appealing to the loyalty of his followers, and shouting over and over again: 'I'm a free citizen of a free state!' The man was surrounded and killed according to instructions, and his Aeduan escort returned to camp.

Labienus remained on the Continent with three legions and 2,000 cavalry: he was to guard the two ports, arrange food supplies, and keep an eye upon events in Gaul. Other measures were left to his discretion. Shortly before sunset[1] I sailed with five legions and 2,000 cavalry; there was a light south-west wind, but about midnight it dropped. The tide carried us right off our course, and at dawn the coast of Britain appeared receding on our port quarter. As soon as the tide turned we rowed hard with it so as to make that part of the island where the best landing points were found last year. The soldiers worked splendidly, and by continuous rowing they enabled the heavily laden transports to keep up with the warships. The whole fleet reached Britain at about noon, but the enemy was nowhere to be seen. We therefore disembarked and chose a site for the camp. Some prisoners revealed that a large native force had originally concentrated on the beaches, but had withdrawn and hidden themselves at Bigbury Woods (*in superiora loca*) when they saw the numbers of our fleet. More than 800 ships, indeed, must have been visible at once, if one included those which had survived last year's expedition and some privately owned vessels. We began moving inland just after midnight, leaving ten battalions and 300 cavalry under Quintus Atrius to guard the fleet. No anxiety was felt about the ships, as they lay at anchor on a nice open shore. A night march of about twelve miles brought us to the Great Stour (*ad flumen*) within sight of the enemy

1. Probably 6 July 54 B.C.

forces. They came down with cavalry and war chariots and, by attacking from higher ground, tried to bar our passage of the river. Repulsed by our cavalry, they retired on the woods where they had a strongly fortified position of great natural strength. It had no doubt been prepared for some war among themselves, for every entrance was blocked by a mass of felled trees. Scattered parties of them came out to fight, and tried to prevent us breaking into the defences; but troops of the Seventh Legion, working under cover of interlocked shields, piled up lumber against the fortifications, stormed the position, and drove them from the woods at the cost of only a few minor casualties. I would not allow them to pursue far: the ground was unfamiliar, and I was anxious to use the few remaining hours of daylight for entrenching the camp. Early next day, however, a light force of infantry and cavalry was sent out in three columns to overtake the fugitives. They had gone some way, and only their rearguard was visible, when some troopers arrived with news from Atrius. It appeared that a great storm overnight had wrecked nearly all the ships or cast them ashore: the anchors and cables had parted, seamen and pilots had been helpless, and heavy damage had been suffered as a result of collision.

After giving orders for the recall of our task force I went back to the coast, and found the news only too true: about 40 ships were a total loss: the remainder could be repaired, but it would mean a very big job. Skilled workmen were called out from the legions, others were summoned from Gaul, and I wrote to Labienus directing him to build as many ships as he could with the troops at his disposal. Meanwhile it was decided to have all vessels beached and enclosed with the camp in a single line of fortifications: it seemed the best thing to do in spite of the enormous labour involved. Actually the job took ten days to complete with the men working day and night.

As soon as the ships were beached and the camp strongly fortified I returned inland, leaving the same guard as before, and on arrival discovered that larger British forces had assembled under Cassivellaunus. This chieftain's territory lies some seventy-five miles from the sea, and is divided from the coastal districts by the river Thames. Until then he had been almost continually at war with the other tribes, but owing to the general alarm inspired by our arrival they had unanimously agreed to confer upon him the supreme command.[1]

The enemy horse and chariots engaged in a fierce running fight with our cavalry, but we had the better of them everywhere and forced them back with heavy casualties into the woods and hills. We suffered a few losses, too, in consequence of a reckless pursuit.

It was not long, however, before the Britons caught us off our guard during the work of entrenchment. They rushed unexpectedly from the woods, attacked the outposts which were stationed in front of the camp, and some heavy fighting ensued. The first and second battalions of two legions went to the rescue, and took up positions quite close together; but the troops were unnerved by these strange tactics, and the enemy with amazing dash broke through the gap and retreated to safety. They were eventually driven off by throwing in more battalions. That day Quintus Laberius Durus, one of our battalion commanders, lost his life.

Throughout this peculiar engagement, which took place in full view of the camp, it was evident that our troops

1. Three chapters, xii-xiv in the Latin, have been omitted as undoubtedly spurious. They describe the state of Britain in the first century B.C.

were too heavily armed: they could not follow up when their opponents gave ground, and they dared not abandon their regular formation. The cavalry, too, had an extremely dangerous task. Every now and then the charioteers fell back on purpose, drew them away from the legions, then jumped down and re-engaged them on foot with the odds heavily in their own favour. Besides, they never fought in close order, but always in wide open formation with reserves posted at strategic points, so that one unit covered another's retreat and fresh, vigorous men took the place of their exhausted comrades.

Next day the enemy took up a position on the hills some considerable distance from the camp. Small groups appeared and began to harass our cavalry, though with not quite the same spirit as on the previous day. However, I had sent out a foraging party consisting of three legions under a general officer, Caius Trebonius, and at midday the natives made a concerted attack, pressing right up to the companies on guard. The latter repulsed them in a furious counter-attack, and maintained pressure until the cavalry, heartened by the sight of the legions, who were moving up to their support, made a charge which drove the Britons in headlong flight and gave them no chance to close their ranks, to stand firm, or to jump from their chariots. In consequence of this defeat, reinforcements sent by the neighbouring tribes dispersed, and the Britons never again fought us in a general action.

On learning the enemy's plan, we moved up in full strength to the Thames, preparatory to entering Cassivellaunus's dominions. The river can be forded at only one point, and even there the crossing was difficult. Large native forces appeared in battle order on the far bank, which was also defended by a line of pointed stakes; and some deserters in our custody revealed that more of these obstacles were planted under water in the river-bed. The cavalry were sent over first, the infantry being ordered to follow soon afterwards; but the legionaries dashed through with such speed (though only their heads were above water), that they were over as soon as the mounted troops. The Britons, overpowered by this combined attack, fled from the bank.

Cassivellaunus had now given up the idea of fighting a pitched battle. He disbanded most of his forces, and followed our line of march with some 4,000 chariots. Keep-

ing off the main route under cover of dense thickets, he drove the inhabitants and their cattle from the open country into the woods wherever he knew that we should pass. If our cavalry ranged too far to plunder and devastate the neighbourhood they were in grave danger from native chariots sent out from the woods to engage them. In face of this threat they could not go far afield: I was obliged to keep them in touch with the main column and be content with such damage as we could do by ravaging and burning the countryside within reach of the legions.

Meanwhile envoys had arrived from the Trinovantes, who were about the strongest tribe in that area. One of their princes, a young man named Mandubracius, had come over to the Continent and put himself under my protection: he had fled for his life when his father, King of the Trinovantes, was assassinated by Cassivellaunus. The envoys promised submission and obedience to my orders: they asked me to defend Mandubracius against the malice of Cassivellaunus, and to send him back as independent ruler of his people. I demanded forty hostages and a supply of grain for the troops. These were promptly delivered, and Mandubracius returned home.

When it became known that the Trinovantes were securely protected and suffered no harm from our troops, five more tribes from southern and eastern Britain (*Cenimagni, Segontiaci, Ancalites, Bibroci, Cassi*) sent delegations and submitted. They told me we were not far from Cassivellaunus's stronghold, which was strategically placed among woods and marshland, and that large numbers of men and cattle were gathered there.

Incidentally the Britons call a 'stronghold' any densely wooded spot fortified with a rampart and trench and used as a refuge against attack by marauding bands.

I started for this place with the legions, and notwithstanding its superb natural defences, which had been improved by strong fortifications, we proceeded to the assault on two sides. After a very brief resistance the enemy gave way and escaped on another side. Great quantities of cattle were found there, and many of the fugitives were overtaken and killed.

During these operations Cassivellaunus sent envoys to the four Kentish rulers, Cingetorix, Carvilius, Taximagulus, and Legovax, directing them to make a surprise assault on our naval base. As soon as their forces appeared the garrison attacked from the gates, killed many of them, took prisoner one of their leaders, a chieftain named Lugotorix, and retired without loss. The news of this engagement found Cassivellaunus already perturbed by his many reverses, by the devastation of his country, and above all by the defection of his allies. Acting through Commius, he sent a delegation to discuss terms of surrender. I had decided to winter on the Continent for fear of sudden risings in Gaul; besides, summer was nearly over, and it was clear that the enemy could easily hold out for the rest of the campaigning season: so I demanded hostages, fixed the annual tribute payable from Britain into the Roman treasury, and strictly forbade Cassivellaunus to interfere with Mandubracius and the Trinovantes. After receiving these hostages we returned to the coast. The ships had been repaired and were now launched; but since we had numerous prisoners, and some vessels had become a total loss in the recent storm, I decided to make the return voyage in two trips. It is worth noting that of the large fleets which had made so many voyages in the past twelve months not one ship with troops on board was lost. As for the empty vessels, which included those on their way back from Gaul after disembarking the first contingent, and the 60 ships newly constructed under Labienus's supervision, very few of them reached their destination: the majority were forced back to land by bad weather. We awaited them for some time in vain, until the approach of the equinox threatened to prevent our sailing at all, and there was nothing for it but to embark in what ships we had, though this necessitated a good deal of overloading. But a dead calm set in; we weighed anchor a little after 9 p.m., and the whole fleet reached land safely at dawn.

That year had been one of drought and grain was scarce, so after beaching the ships and holding the Gallic Diet at Amiens (*Samarobrivae*) I was obliged to establish the legions' winter camps over a wider area than in previous years. Gaius Fabius took one legion to Flanders (*in Morinos*) another, under Quintus Cicero, proceeded to Namur (*in Nervios*); a third was stationed on the Orne (*in Esuvios*) under Lucius Roscius, while Labienus went with another into the Argonne (*in Remis*). Three more legions were quartered around Beauvais, Amiens, and Arras (*in Belgis*), under the chief of staff Marcus Crassus and two generals, Lucius Munatius Plancus and Caius Trebonius, respectively. Sabinus and Cotta, with one newly recruited legion from north of the Po and a detachment of five cohorts, were ordered to Tongres (*in Eburones*) in the dominions of Ambiorix and Catuvolcus, two chieftains of the Eburones, the larger part of whose territory lies between the Meuse and the Rhine.

This wide distribution of the legions seemed the easiest way of dealing with the shortage of grain. The distances between each camp, however, were not excessive; for, with the exception of Roscius, who was going to an absolutely quiet and peaceful area, no commander was more than one hundred miles or so from the next. I decided to remain at Amiens (*in Gallia*) until I was satisfied that all troops had reached their destinations and had fortified their camps.

Among the Carnutes was a man of noble birth named Tasgetius. His ancestors had once been kings of that tribe, and in recognition of his ability and personal devotion to me—he had rendered most useful service in all our campaigns—I had restored him to his ancestral dignity. In the third year of his reign he was assassinated by a group of private enemies, though with the open approval of many of his subjects. The news was disquieting: a good many people were implicated in this crime, and it was possible they might persuade the whole tribe to revolt. I therefore instructed Plancus to move at once with a single legion into Carnutian territory on the middle Loire (*in Carnutes*), and to spend the winter there. He had orders to arrest and send to my headquarters those responsible for the murder of Tasgetius. Meanwhile I was informed by the commanding officers of the various legions that they had reached their camps and completed the fortifications.

Roman Disaster at Tongres

ABOUT a fortnight later trouble began at the instigation of the Eburonian rulers, Ambiorix and Catuvolcus. They had waited upon Sabinus and Cotta at the frontier, and supplied a certain amount of grain; but a message from the Treveran chief, Indutiomarus, now caused them to raise the standard of revolt. They made a sudden attack on a party of troops gathering wood, overpowered them, and came on in force against the Roman camp. The men quickly armed and mounted the rampart, whilst a troop of Spanish horse rode out from one of the gates and fought a successful engagement. The enemy, realizing they had no chance of victory, retired; but, in accordance with tribal custom, they began shouting for someone on our side to come out and confer with them. They professed to have something of mutual interest to discuss whereby, they felt sure, all differences could be resolved. Two delegates were sent, Caius Arpireius, a Roman knight and a personal friend of Sabinus, and one Quintus Junius, a Spaniard whom I had already employed on several missions to Ambiorix. The following is an outline of Ambiorix's address:

1. He acknowledged his indebtedness to me for having
   (a) relieved him from the tribute he had once paid to the neighbouring Atuatuci;
   (b) restored to him his son and nephew, both of whom had been sent as hostages to the Atuatuci and then kept in chains as slaves.

2. He stated that the attack on the Roman camp had been made against his advice and contrary to his wishes. His subjects had forced his hand: he was only nominal ruler of a people who had as much, if not more, authority than he. The reason for their hostility was that they could not oppose a united Gallic league which had been sprung on them without warning. His own insignificance proved this; for he was not such a fool as to imagine that his unaided forces could overwhelm the might of Rome. The fact was that the Gauls had unanimously appointed that day for a simultaneous attack on all the winter camps so as to prevent the legions helping one another. It was hard for Gauls to refuse co-operation with their fellow countrymen, especially when the object was to win back the freedom of their race.

3. He said that, having done his duty as a patriot, he remembered what he owed to me, and urgently requested Sabinus as his friend and former guest to consult his own safety and that of the men under his command. A large force of German mercenaries had crossed the Rhine and would arrive in two days: it was for Sabinus to decide whether it would not be wise to withdraw his troops before the surrounding tribes discovered what was afoot, and to join Cicero 50 miles distant, or Labienus who was stationed somewhat farther away. He swore to give them a safe conduct through his own dominions, and pointed out that in making this offer he was acting in the interests of his people by relieving them of the presence of Roman troops, and at the same time repaying me a debt of gratitude.

Ambiorix then withdrew, and the delegates reported back to their commanding officers, who were alarmed by this unexpected development. The proposal itself could not be altogether ignored, coming though it did from an enemy source; but the situation was aggravated by the incredible audacity of an obscure and insignificant tribe making war on its own initiative against Rome. The matter was accordingly referred to a council of war, where there was considerable difference of opinion. Cotta was supported by a number of company commanders and senior centurions in opposing a hasty decision. He pointed out that it would be most irregular to abandon the camp without authority from the commander-in-chief, and insisted that the fortifications were strong enough to hold an attack by any number of Gallic levies and a large force of Germans as well. In support of this view he recalled the splendid resistance which beat off the first attack and inflicted heavy casualties. He emphasized that there was no food shortage, and argued that, before such an emergency could arise, relief would come from headquarters as well as from the neighbouring camps. He maintained, finally, that to take the enemy's advice in questions affecting high strategy would argue a disgraceful lack of judgment and common sense.

Against this view Sabinus protested that it would be too late to do anything at all once the Eburones had been reinforced and had made contact with these German mercenaries, and any disaster to the neighbouring camps would be equally fatal. Time was short, he urged, and it was more than likely that the commander-in-chief had already started for Italy: if he were still in Gaul the Carnutes would never have decided upon the murder of Tasgetius, nor would the Eburones have held the Roman force in such contempt as to make an attack on its camp. It was not a question, he continued, of being guided by the enemy, but by hard facts: the Rhine was not far away; the Germans had been embittered by the death of Ariovistus and by Roman victories in earlier campaigns; the Gauls were burning with anger at the many humiliations to which they had been subjected under Roman rule and at the eclipse of their ancient military renown. Moreover it was inconceivable that Ambiorix would have adopted his present line unless he were quite sure of success. Sabinus then argued that his own proposal was safe either way: if there were no immediate danger, no risk would attend a march to link up with troops in the next camp; whereas if Gaul were united and in league with the Germans, speed alone offered a chance of escape. He concluded by affirming that the plan recommended by Cotta and his supporters could have only one result, irrespective of the danger here and now—a protracted siege and death by starvation.

Cotta and the centurions remained firmly opposed to this alternative. 'Very well, have your own way then,' cried Sabinus, raising his voice so that many of the troops could hear him. 'I am the last man to be scared of death. But remember, the men are no fools: if things go wrong they will hold you responsible. After all, if you would only agree, the day after to-morrow would find them ready for anything alongside their comrades in the next camp, not cut off here in complete isolation waiting for death by famine or cold steel.'

The members now rose from the council table: they gathered round the two generals and implored them not to persist in a quarrel which must have fatal consequences. All would be well, they pleaded, whether they went or stayed, provided there was unanimity of thought and action: bickering would mean disaster. The debate, however, continued until nearly midnight, when Cotta was finally overruled and Sabinus's plan adopted. An order of the day was issued announcing that the troops would leave at dawn.

The men took no sleep that night: every one was looking through his kit to see what he could take with him and how much of his winter equipment he would have to leave behind. All tried hard to convince themselves that it really was dangerous to remain, and that the danger would be aggravated by weariness inseparable from the long watches that would be necessary.

At daybreak they started in a long, straggling column with a good deal of transport, just as if they believed that the enemy who had suggested the plan was their devoted friend. The natives heard sounds during the night, realized that the men had not turned in, and guessed that they intended to leave. A double ambush was concealed at strategic points in the woods some two miles from the camp and waited for the Roman column to approach. The main body had made its way down into a great ravine, when the enemy suddenly appeared at either end, fell on the rearguard, and barred the road leading up from the defile.

From Sabinus's point of view the scene of action could not have been worse. He had anticipated nothing like this: he lost his head, and ran up and down the line trying to get the troops into some sort of battle formation. But his nerves had gone to pieces and he was clearly at his wits' end. That, of course, always happens when an officer has to make his plans after the battle has started. Cotta, however, had imagined something of the kind happening on the march: that, indeed, was partly his reason for rejecting the whole scheme; but he was equal to the emergency, handling the men as if he were their supreme commander, and fighting like a private soldier. The length of the column made it impossible for the two generals to attend to everything personally and at every point, so they had word passed down to abandon the transport, and form a circle. All things considered one cannot altogether condemn this decision, but it had most unfortunate consequences: it lowered our soldiers' morale besides encouraging the enemy, who took it as a sign of panic and despair. Inevitably, too, there were many cases of troops leaving the ranks to save their treasured possessions from the baggage; and everywhere there were confused uproar and frantic cries.

The natives, however, were fully alive to the situation: orders were given that no one was to leave the ranks. The men were assured that any materials abandoned by the Romans were common property, and every one would get his share; but for the moment all must concentrate on winning the battle. Luck was against our troops, and their commander had failed them: nevertheless they fought with desperate courage, and whenever they charged, the enemy suffered heavy casualties. Ambiorix now ordered his men to hurl their weapons from a distance and avoid hand-to-hand fighting: their light armour and constant training would enable them to withdraw in good time before a Roman attack, and they would counter-attack as the legionaries regrouped. These instructions were obeyed to the letter: any battalion charging from the circle offered an exposed flank to a hail of missiles, and on turning to regain its original position was in danger of being caught between the enemy units that had fallen back and those at either extremity of the gap. If the legionaries attempted merely to hold their ground as part of the circle, they had no room to show their fighting qualities; and they were so closely packed as to offer a sitting target for the storm of javelins hurled by that tremendous host. But notwithstanding all these handicaps and their heavy losses, they stood firm. It was now 2 p.m.; the action had lasted since dawn, and during the whole of that time they had lived up to their

finest traditions. Titus Balventius, a brave and highly respected officer, who was chief centurion of his legion a year
ago, had both thighs pierced by a javelin. Another centurion of the same grade, Quintus Lucanius, was killed in
a very gallant attempt to rescue his own son who had been
surrounded. Cotta himself was wounded by a sling-stone,
which struck him full in the face as he moved through the
ranks cheering his men.

Sabinus was so alarmed by this turn of events that, when
he caught sight of Ambiorix directing the action some way

off, he sent his interpreter, Gnaeus Pom-
peius, to ask for quarter for himself and
his troops. In answer to this appeal Ambiorix consented to discuss terms: he expressed a hope that his people might
agree to spare the men's lives; in any case,
he would give his personal assurance that
Sabinus should come to no harm. As
Cotta was wounded, Sabinus proposed
that they should both leave the battle and
together confer with Ambiorix, from
whom he expected to obtain generous
conditions for their two selves and for
the legion. But Cotta flatly refused to
wait upon an enemy who carried arms,
and Sabinus accordingly told the nearest
battalion commanders and senior centurions to follow him. As he approached
Ambiorix he was told to lay down his
arms: he did so and ordered his compa-
nions to do the same. During negotiations, which the Gaul
intentionally prolonged, Sabinus was gradually surrounded
and then murdered. The natives immediately raised their

usual shout of triumph, and, with a loud yell, rushed in and broke the Roman ranks. Cotta fell fighting, and most of the troops with him. The survivors took refuge in their camp. One of them, the standard-bearer Lucius Petrosidius, was cut off by a crowd of natives: he threw the eagle inside the palisade, and died a hero's death before the rampart. The rest managed to hold out till darkness fell; but during the night, since the position was manifestly hopeless, every one of them died by his comrade's hand. A small group had escaped during the engagement, and after wandering aimlessly through the woods they reached Labienus's camp and told him what had happened.

Attack on Cicero's Camp

ELATED by this success, Ambiorix set out at once with an escort of cavalry and directed his infantry to follow. Riding day and night, he reached the adjoining district of Hesbaye (*in Atuatucos*), where he roused the enthusiasm of the Atuatuci with news of his achievement. Next day he continued westward into Brabant (*in Nervios*) and urged the Nervii not to lose this opportunity of regaining their freedom and avenging the many sufferings they had endured under Roman rule. Two generals, he announced, had been killed, and most of their army wiped out: it would be a simple matter to surprise Cicero's winter camp and annihilate his legion also. The Nervii gladly accepted his offer to assist them in this undertaking, and ordered their dependent tribes (*Ceutrones, Grudios, Levacos, Pleumoxios, Geidumnos*) to press every man they could into service. These forces were assembled and marched on Cicero's camp before he received news of Sabinus's death. Once again some of his men were absent in the woods collecting timber for repair work on the fortifications: they were naturally cut off by the unexpected arrival of the enemy's cavalry and surrounded. Before long the Eburones, Nervii, and Atuatuci, supported by their respective allies and satellites, launched an attack on the camp in enormous strength. The troops ran to arms and mounted the rampart, and there was some extremely bitter fighting that day; for the enemy were relying on speed, and believed that successs in this engagement would be the guarantee of final victory.

Cicero wrote to me without delay, and offered his couriers very substantial rewards if they managed to get through with his dispatch, but all the roads were blocked and they were intercepted. During the night about 120 towers were constructed with incredible speed from timber that had been collected for use on the defences, and all weak points in the fortifications were repaired.

By next day the enemy had been strongly reinforced. They renewed the assault and filled up the ditch, but our fellows offered the same dogged resistance. Similar attacks were launched on several successive days, and work had to continue all night, so that there was no chance of sleep even for the sick and wounded. Whatever was wanted for the next day's fighting was prepared overnight, including large numbers of siege-pikes and fire-hardened stakes. Additional storeys were built on to the towers and covered with a crenellated breastwork of hurdles. Cicero himself was in very poor health, but he refused to take any rest even at night, until the men actually crowded round him and made him promise not to overtax his strength.

A few of the Nervian chieftains and military leaders had some sort of claim on Cicero's friendship, which gave them right of audience. They asked for, and were granted, an interview, in the course of which they covered the same ground as Ambiorix had done with Sabinus: the whole of Gaul was in arms; the Germans had crossed the Rhine; all the winter camps and the commander-in-chief's own headquarters were besieged. They also told him of Sabinus's end, and cited the presence of Ambiorix as proof of their credibility. They assured him that he was greatly mistaken if he expected help from other commanders, who were extremely worried about their own affairs; but they insisted that their only quarrel with Cicero and with Rome generally was the choice of their territory as winter quarters for the legions. They were quite ready to co-operate in all other respects, but the prospect of these camps becoming regular establishments was intolerable. They proposed to grant a safe conduct through their dominions if Cicero would withdraw his troops: this would mean that the legion could begin marching without the slightest fear in any direction they chose. Cicero's reply was brief and to the point. 'Rome,' he said, 'never accepts terms from an enemy in arms against her: if you lay down your arms and send representatives to my commander-in-chief I will support your request, to which you may be assured he will listen with his invariable sense of fair play.'

After this rebuff the Nervii proceeded to encircle the camp with a 10-foot wall and a trench about 15 feet wide. They had learned something of Roman siege operations by observing our methods in previous years, and had obtained further advice on the subject from some Roman prisoners. They lacked the proper tools for such work, and had to cut sods with their swords, excavate earth with their hands, and carry it away in their cloaks. One can, however, get some idea of their numbers from the fact that in less than three hours they threw up a line of earthworks nearly three miles in circumference. They devoted the next few days to the construction of siege-towers and the preparation of grappling-irons and mantlets—all, of course, under the direction of Roman prisoners of war.

On the seventh day of the siege a furious gale blew up, the enemy now began slinging heated bullets made of plastic clay and hurling red-hot darts on to the sheds. These buildings were thatched, as they usually are in Gaul: the straw was quickly alight, and the flames, driven by the wind, spread all over the camp. The natives imagined victory as already in their grasp: they raised a tremendous shout, moved up their towers and mantlets, and attempted to scale the rampart by means of ladders. But the cool courage of our troops was magnificent. They were engulfed in scorching heat under a rain of missiles, and it was obvious that the whole of their equipment, containing all their possessions, would be destroyed. Yet not a single man deserted his post, and scarcely one so much as looked behind him. They all fought splendidly. Their situation indeed had never been more grave; but in spite of that the enemy lost more killed and wounded that day than on any other, for the Gallic host had crowded together under the fortifications, and their rear ranks prevented the withdrawal of those in front.

As the fire began to die down an enemy siege-tower was moved up at one point until it actually touched the rampart: whereupon the centurions of the third battalion moved back, ordered their men to do likewise, and invited the natives by voice and gesture to come on inside if they wished. But none of them dared move: they were dislodged with volleys of stones from all directions, and their tower was set on fire.

There were two splendid fellows in that legion, Titus Pullo and Lucius Vorenus, both of them centurions and both nearly qualified for the first grade. They were for ever arguing over their respective merits, and every year found them at loggerheads in the race for promotion. At the height of this action Pullo suddenly remarked: 'Come on, Vorenus, what are you waiting for? We'll finish that argument to-day.' He immediately left the shelter of the rampart and made a dash for the thickest point he could find in the enemy ranks. Vorenus, of course, was after him in a moment: his reputation was seriously challenged. At quite short range Pullo hurled his pike, which went clean through one of the Gallic soldiers as he rushed forward: the man fell unconscious, but his comrades covered him with their shields, and at the same time directed a hail of fire at Pullo, who could therefore go no farther. A javelin then penetrated his shield, lodged in his belt, and knocked the scabbard out of place. The result was that he could not reach his sword in time, and in that unpleasant predicament he was surrounded. Vorenus hurried to the rescue, and at once the whole mob turned on him. He laid about him with his sword, fighting at close quarters, killed one man, and drove the rest back a little. But he was just a bit too keen, and tumbled headlong into a dip in the ground where he in turn was surrounded. This time Pullo was the saviour, and after killing quite a few of the enemy they both got back to camp covered in glory. Fortune had certainly teased these two in their bitter rivalry: yet, for all their mutual hostility, each owed his life to the other, and no one could really say who deserved the prize.

It became increasingly difficult to sustain the siege with its attendant hardships, particularly since many of the troops had been wounded and the defenders reduced to a mere handful of men. As the situation deteriorated Cicero redoubled his efforts to get a dispatch through to me: some of his couriers were stopped almost at once and tortured to death in full view of the rampart. But there was a Nervian in the camp, a man of good birth named Vertico, who had deserted to Cicero at the very beginning of the siege and had served him faithfully ever since. This man, by promising his slave freedom and a large sum of money, persuaded him to carry a dispatch to my headquarters. He took it out wound round his spear, and as he was a Gaul moving among fellow Gauls he managed to get through without arousing suspicion. In this way I heard of the danger threatening Cicero and his legion. The dispatch reached me early in the evening, and I immediately sent a courier to my chief of staff, Marcus Crassus, who was stationed not far from Beauvais (*in Bellovacos*) about twenty-four miles away, ordering him to start at midnight with his legion and join me with all possible speed. He left as soon as this message arrived. Another courier was sent to Gaius Fabius, instructing him to proceed in full strength to the neighbourhood of Arras (*in Atrebates*) through which I should have to pass. Written instructions to Labienus directed him to move his troops to the Nervian frontier north-east of St. Quentin (*ad fines Nerviorum*), but only if he could do so without risk. The remaining legions were too far away, and it seemed best not to await their arrival: but some 400 cavalry were summoned from the nearest camps.

At about nine o'clock next morning I was notified by Crassus's forward patrols that he was approaching. I left him in command at Amiens with one legion to guard the military stores, the native hostages, the state archives, and the granaries. Fabius meanwhile had obeyed his instructions: he joined me on the road soon afterwards, and we covered about twenty miles before nightfall. Labienus, however, had news of the disaster that had overtaken Sabinus and his force. The Treveri had moved against him in full strength, and he was convinced that his withdrawal would have the appearance of retreat. He knew they were jubilant over the recent Gallic success, and feared it would be impossible to deal with them if they attacked his force in column of route. He therefore wrote back explaining the grave risk that his departure would involve, gave me a full account of Sabinus's engagement with the Eburones, and stated that the whole Treveran army was already encamped three miles from his own position.

It was disappointing to be reduced to only two legions, one less than I had expected; but Labienus's decision was undoubtedly right. Speed was now essential: we reached the neighbourhood of Cambrai (*in Nerviorum fines*) by a series of forced marches, and were informed by some Nervian prisoners of Cicero's predicament.

I bribed one of our Gallic horsemen to take a message to Cicero: it was written in Greek characters so as to leave the enemy none the wiser if it were intercepted. In the event of his being unable to get into the camp, he was to throw it over the rampart tied to the thong of his spear. The letter informed Cicero that I was on my way with two legions and would be with him shortly, and it urged him to continue holding on for all he was worth. The Gaul took no chances; but he followed instructions, and flung in the spear. It stuck, quite accidentally, in the woodwork of a tower, and remained there unnoticed for two days. Then one of the men saw it, drew it out, and delivered it to Cicero who, after glancing through it, read it out to the troops on parade. They were overjoyed; and when, very soon afterwards, the smoke of burning villages was seen in the distance, they knew for certain that relief was at hand.

The Gauls were informed of our approach by their patrols. They raised the siege and turned off to meet us in full
strength—about 60,000 men. Cicero once again asked Vertico for the use of his Gallic runner: this second dispatch
advised me to proceed with the utmost caution, as the
enemy had diverted their troops to intercept the relief
force. Directly his letter reached me, about midnight, I had
the men told of its contents, and an order of the day warned
them that all their courage would be required in the fighting that lay ahead. We struck camp at dawn, and after
marching about four miles came in view of the enemy host
on the opposite side of a broad valley through which flowed
a stream. The ground was unfavourable, and it would have
been most dangerous to engage there and then with the
small forces at my disposal. Besides, there was no cause
for anxiety: Cicero was no longer blockaded, and there
was plenty of time. We therefore halted and began entrenching a camp on the best available site. It would have
been small enough in any case, for there were barely 7,000
troops and no transport; but its area was limited still further
by reducing the width of all roadways so as to make our
numbers appear ridiculously small. Meanwhile scouts were
detailed to find the most convenient path across the valley.
Apart from some insignificant cavalry skirmishes along
the water's edge, neither side moved from its position: the
enemy was expecting reinforcements, and I wanted to see
whether they could be drawn by pretence of fear. If so, we
should be able to fight on our own ground in front of the
camp; if not, then a complete survey of the route would
at least enable us to cross both valley and stream with a
minimum of risk. Next day, at dawn, the Gallic horse
came over and engaged our cavalry whom I purposely
directed to fall back on the camp. The legionaries, mean-

while, were ordered to raise the entire circuit of our defences, to barricade the gates, and to do it all with as much
show of panic and confusion as they could.

The enemy fell into the trap: they came over in strength
and took up an unfavourable position. I then ordered the
troops to stand away from the rampart, and they came still
nearer: javelins were hurled into the camp, and heralds
went round the fortifications proclaiming that any one,
Gaul or Roman, might come and join them before nine
o'clock, after which there would be no admittance. The
barricades were, in point of fact, mere imitations, each
consisting of no more than a single thickness of turf. The
Gauls, however, decided they could not break in by the
gates: utterly contemptuous of our strength, they began
filling up the trenches and tried to pull down the palisade
with their bare hands. While the legions raced from all
four exits, I ordered a sudden charge of cavalry and the
natives fled. There was absolutely no resistance whatever:
many of them were killed and the survivors threw away
their arms, but the vicinity of woods and marshland made
it unsafe to pursue for any distance.

We had suffered no casualties, and therefore pushed on
to Cicero's camp, where I was truly amazed by the Gallic
siege-works. A review of his troops showed that less than
one-tenth of the men remained unwounded, and I con-
gratulated him and the whole legion on their magnificent
courage in handling a most dangerous situation. Individual
praise went to battalion commanders and centurions whom
Cicero had named as having specially distinguished themselves. After learning more about the fate of Sabinus and
Cotta from some prisoners of war, I paraded the troops
next day, gave them particulars of the disaster, and reassured
them. 'The whole thing,' I said, 'was due to the damned

inefficiency of Sabinus. You have no need to be upset: Providence and your own gallantry have restored the balance; the enemy's triumph was very short. Now forget about it.'

News of our success was brought to Labienus by a party of Remi with incredible speed. He was about fifty-seven  miles from Cicero's camp, which I had not reached until just before 2 p.m.; yet before midnight shouts were heard at the gates, and there they were, announcing a Roman victory and offering the congratulations of their tribe. The Treveran commander Indutiomarus had decided to launch his attack on Labienus's position next day, but on receiving this news he made off during the night with his whole army. Fabius was ordered back to his quarters with one legion, while I settled three more in separate camps around Amiens, and in view of the serious unrest in Gaul I decided to stay with the army for the rest of that winter.

The Gallic victory over Sabinus had set practically all the native states talking of war: they were exchanging envoys over a wide area in an endeavour to learn one another's plans and to find someone who would take the initiative. Secret gatherings were being held by night in lonely spots, and throughout those winter months I was rarely free from anxiety. Scarcely a day passed without my receiving word of some Gallic intrigue or troop movements: for example, a report from the quarter-master-general, Roscius, commanding the Thirteenth Legion, stated that large forces of the so-called Armorican tribes on the north-western seaboard had concentrated about eight miles from his camp preparatory to making an attack; but the announcement of our success had been followed immediately by a somewhat precipitate withdrawal. I managed, however, to hold a majority of the states to their allegiance by summoning their chieftains to my headquarters: pressure was needed to bring some of them, others took a courteous hint. But one of the strongest and most influential of the tribes—the Senones, on the lower Yonne—planned to assassinate their ruler Cavarinus. I had set this man on his ancestral throne in succession to his brother Maritasgus, who had occupied it at the time of my first arrival in Gaul. He got wind of the plot and escaped, but was pursued to the frontier, dethroned, and exiled. The Senones then sent a delegation to excuse their conduct, but subsequently disobeyed my orders which required the presence of their whole tribal council.

The truth was that someone had appeared to lead them in offensive warfare, and this fact had made so deep an impression upon these simple native peoples, and had so entirely changed their outlook, that almost every tribe was under suspicion in our eyes. The only exceptions were the Aedui, whom I had always held in great esteem for their long-standing record of unswerving loyalty, and the Remi, who had served us well in recent campaigns. This tendency to revolt is perhaps less surprising when one considers its many underlying causes, and in particular the resentment felt by men who had once been regarded as second to none in courage and fighting skill, but had now so far lost their ancient prestige as to admit the sovereignty of Rome.

Indutiomarus and the Treveri were active throughout the winter, sending delegations beyond the Rhine, intriguing with the German states, promising them money, and assuring them that the Roman army had become a negligible factor in consequence of its enormous losses. But none of these tribes could be induced to cross the Rhine: their experiences in the campaigns of Ariovistus and the migration of the Tencteri, they said, had decided them not to tempt fortune a third time.

Notwithstanding his disappointment, however, Indutiomarus went ahead with his plans, training new levies, buying up horses from the surrounding tribes, and, by means of liberal pay, attracting to his standard a host of condemned criminals and exiles from all over Gaul. His fame and authority were now such that he received deputations from many different quarters, requesting his favour and alliance on behalf of their governments or of individual chiefs. In the light of these unsolicited overtures he saw there would be no lack of support if he advanced beyond his own frontiers: south-west the Carnutes and Senones were drifting to revolt through a sense of guilt in the matter of Tasgetius and Caravinus; westward the Nervii and Atuatuci were already making preparations for war with Rome. He therefore gave notice of an armed convention, the usual prelude to hostilities in Gaul. A law common to all the tribes requires the attendance of all adult males: they must come armed, and the last to arrive is tortured to death before the whole assembly. Indutiomarus opened the convention by declaring his son-in-law Cingetorix a public enemy, and confiscated his property. This man, it will be remembered, was the leader of a rival party, who had put himself under my protection and remained consistently loyal. The assembly was next informed that the Senones, Carnutes, and other Gallic states had asked for help: Indutiomarus announced his intention of giving assistance and of devastating Champagne (*fines Remorum*) on the way. But he intended first to storm Labienus's camp, and proceeded to outline his plans for that operation.

Labienus was perfectly safe in a camp strongly fortified by nature as well as by human art. He felt no anxiety for himself or his men; his only concern was to fight a successful engagement at the earliest possible moment. He obtained from Cingetorix and his family an account of Indutiomarus's address to the convention, and immediately sent orders to the neighbouring tribes to furnish a number of mounted contingents by an appointed date. Meanwhile Indutiomarus and his cavalry rode slowly round the fortifications almost every day, either to reconnoitre the site, or to get a few words with our troops, or simply to frighten them. As a rule these horsemen flung their spears over the rampart, but Labienus kept his men close within their lines, doing his best to appear thoroughly alarmed. The Gallic commander continued these daily visits, but began to show increasing contempt for his opponent. One night Labienus managed to bring in all his fresh native cavalry. He posted his sentries so carefully that no one could leave the camp, no leakage of information was possible, and the Treveri remained ignorant of these reinforcements.

Eventually Indutiomarus came over on one of his routine patrols and spent most of the day there while his men flung their javelins and a good deal of foul abuse into the bargain, hoping thereby to force an engagement. They got no reply, and towards evening moved off at their leisure in scattered groups. Labienus seized that moment to hurl his cavalry from two gates: they had strict orders that once the enemy had panicked (as he foresaw they would) and were properly on the run, every man was to concentrate on finding Indutiomarus. The rest could wait until it was absolutely certain their leader was dead: no time must be wasted on any one else—it would only give him a chance to escape. There was a big price on his head, and to make sure he did not get away some infantry battalions were sent out in support.

Fortune favoured her devoted Labienus: with every one searching for him, Indutiomarus was caught and killed in the act of fording a stream. His head was brought back to camp, and on their return journey the cavalry rounded up and slaughtered as many as they could. The combined Nervian-Eburonian forces disbanded as soon as they heard this news, and Gaul was thenceforward more peaceful.

BOOK SIX

[53 B.C.]

General Sedition in Gaul

THERE were several reasons for expecting worse trouble in Gaul, and three members of my staff, Marcus Silanus, Gaius Antistius Regenus, and Titus Sextius, were commissioned to enrol fresh troops. Pompey was then in the neighbourhood of Rome: he had been given proconsular power with military command, but was staying in Italy for political reasons. During his consulship [55 B.C.] he had sworn in a number of recruits in Cisalpine Gaul, and I now asked him to call up these men and send them out to join me. It was desirable to impress public opinion in Gaul by showing that Italy's manpower was sufficient not only to make good our losses in the field, but even to increase the size of our armies on foreign service. Pompey acceded to this request; the commissioners were not long in raising further levies, and three new legions—more than twice the number of battalions lost by Sabinus—were in due course brought over to Gaul. These very strong reinforcements and the speed with which they were assembled demonstrated what Roman organization and resources could achieve.

145

On the death of Indutiomarus the Treveri had conferred his authority on his next of kin, who persisted in trying to buy German aid. Failing to persuade the nearest tribes, they made offers to more distant states, some of whom agreed to their proposals. Oaths were exchanged; Treveran hostages were given as security for payment; and Ambiorix was admitted to the league. This information and similar reports from elsewhere convinced me that a general outbreak was imminent: the Nervii, Atuatuci, and Menapii together with all the Germanic tribes on the left bank of the Rhine were already in arms; the Senones had ignored my summons and were intriguing with the Carnutes and other nearby groups; and the Treveri were sending one delegation after another to solicit German intervention. It was evident that we should have to think in terms of war earlier than usual.

Winter had not yet ended when I took the four legions nearest to Amiens and made an unexpected descent on Hainaut (*in fines Nerviorum*), giving the Nervii no opportunity to concentrate or to flee. Large herds of cattle and numerous prisoners were taken and handed over to the soldiers for their own use; the countryside was devastated, and the Nervii were obliged to submit and to surrender hostages. That business was quickly settled: the legions returned to winter quarters, and early in the spring I convoked the usual Gallic Diet. Representatives of every tribe attended, except the Senones, Carnutes, and Treveri, whose absence I regarded as a prelude to armed rebellion; and in order to make it clear that everything else was of secondary importance, I adjourned the Diet to Paris (*Lutetiam Parisiorum*) by a decree which was read from the commander's tribunal. The inhabitants of that district were immediate neighbours of the Senones, with whom they had united a generation earlier to form one state. It appeared, however, that they were not implicated in the present affair. I started with the legions on the same day, and entered Senonian territory after a series of forced marches.

Acco, the ringleader of this conspiracy, on learning of our approach directed the population to assemble in their strongholds; but before they could do so the news of our arrival compelled them to abandon the project, and envoys were sent to ask for pardon. Their petition was seconded by the Aedui, under whose protection they had lived from time immemorial, and in deference to whom I willingly accepted their apologies and granted their request. In any case, summer was the campaigning season and no time for holding a judicial inquiry; but I took 300 hostages, who were delivered to the Aedui for safe custody, and then received a delegation from the Carnutes (sponsored by their overlords, the Remi), who were granted similar terms. The Diet then completed its business, and the various states were instructed to provide drafts of cavalry.

The pacification of these areas left me free to devote my whole attention to the campaign against Ambiorix and the Treveri. Cavarinus was ordered to accompany our Senonian horse: a man of hot temper, he had incurred the enmity of his tribe, and might prove a source of trouble on that account. It was certain that Ambiorix would not risk a pitched battle, and the question therefore remained, what other plans he might have. Immediately north of the Eburones lay the Menapii, who were protected by a continuous belt of marsh and forest, and were the only Gallic tribe that had never offered to negotiate with us. I knew that Ambiorix was united to them by ties of hospitality, and also that the Treveri had negotiated a German alliance on his behalf. It seemed advisable first to deprive him of these allies, for a direct attack now might only drive him to seek refuge with the Menapii or to link up with the tribes beyond the Rhine. Accordingly I had all military stores removed to Labienus's camp in the Argonne (*in Treveros*), ordered two legions to join me, and started with five others in light marching order for the Low Countries (*in Menapios*). The Menapii, relying on their natural defences, had assembled no troops: they moved for safety with all their belongings into the forest and marshland areas. Fabius and Marcus Crassus were given command of separate detachments, and our three columns advanced along hastily built causeways, burning farms and villages, seizing large herds of cattle, and taking many prisoners, until the Menapii were obliged to send envoys and sue for peace. After receiving their hostages I warned them that they would be regarded as enemies if they admitted Ambiorix or his agents within their territory; and leaving the Atrebatan Commius with a detachment of cavalry to keep an eye on the situation, I started for the Moselle basin (*in Treveros*) to deal with the Treveri. These people had concentrated powerful forces of both arms preparatory to an attack on Labienus's camp, which was held by a single legion: they were within a couple of days' march of their objective when they heard that another two legions, which I sent to his relief, had crossed the frontier. They encamped at a distance of about fourteen miles to await the arrival of some German reinforcements; but Labienus discovered their plan, and, in the hope that their recklessness would afford him the chance to fight a decisive action, he went to meet them with the equivalent of two and a half legions and a strong force of cavalry, leaving a garrison of five companies to guard his equipment.

He entrenched a position about one mile from the

enemy's camp and on the other side of a river, which was difficult to cross because of its very steep banks: indeed he had no intention of trying, and it seemed improbable that the enemy would do so. Now the Gauls became increasingly confident that they would be reinforced, so Labienus purposely let fall a remark in the men's hearing, that, as the Germans were coming up, he would not endanger himself and his troops, but would strike camp and withdraw next day. His words were quickly repeated to the enemy, for among so many native auxiliaries there were inevitably some who had their fellow countrymen's interest at heart. During the night Labienus summoned his battalion commanders and centurions, outlined his plan, and gave orders for the camp to be broken up with more noise and confusion than is usual with Roman armies. His departure, in fact, bore all the marks of a disorderly retreat; and as the opposing camps were so close to one another, the news was reported to the enemy before daybreak by their patrols. The natives were most anxious not to lose this long-awaited prize; they argued that it was pointless to wait for German help when the Romans were themselves on the run; they felt it would detract from their own prowess, too, if, notwithstanding their great numbers, they hesitated to attack a small enemy force already in retreat and hampered by its transport. The rearguard had scarcely left the entrenchment when the Gauls began boldly swarming over the river to fight on what was really most unfavourable ground. Labienus had expected this and continued moving slowly forward, keeping up his pretence of withdrawal. When they were all across, he sent his transport slightly ahead and had it stationed on some high ground. Then he addressed the troops: 'Soldiers! Now is your chance: you have the enemy in the palm of your hand—in a hopeless

position, where he cannot possibly manœuvre. Show that
spirit under my leadership, which you have so often shown
under the eyes of your commander-in-chief: imagine he
is present looking on. Face about now,' he shouted, 'and

into line!' A few cavalry squadrons were sent to protect
the transport, the remainder rode out on the flanks; and
the men, raising a tremendous cheer, hurled their pikes. The
enemy were appalled to see troops, whom a moment before they had believed in full retreat, racing to the attack.
There was no opposition: directly the lines met the Gauls
turned and ran. They were hunted down by Roman
cavalry, who slaughtered them in masses and took a good
many prisoners. Within a few days Labienus had the tribe
once more under control: for the German reinforcements
made for home as soon as they got news of a Treveran

defeat, and Indutiomarus's relations, who had instigated the rebellion, fled the country with them. Cingetorix's constant loyalty was rewarded with the civil government and military organization of his people.

On reaching Treveran territory from the Low Countries I decided to cross the Rhine, for two reasons: first, because the Germans had sent reinforcements to help the Treveri against us; second, to prevent Ambiorix escaping to Germany. Bridging operations were accordingly started a little above our former crossing, and, as the principle of construction was now quite familiar, were completed within a few days after some hard work on the soldiers' part. Leaving a strong guard on the western bank in case of a sudden Gallic rising, I took over the remaining legionaries and all my cavalry. The Ubii, who had previously given hostages and made their submission, sent envoys to clear themselves. They were emphatic as to their loyalty, and protested that any help received by the Treveri had certainly not come from their state. They implored me to spare them, and not to make innocent men suffer for others' guilt through indiscriminate hatred of all Germans: if I wanted more hostages they would surrender them. Investigations proved that the reinforcements had been sent by the Suebi; and having accepted the Ubii's assurances, I began making inquiries about possible routes into Suebic territory.

Some days later the Ubii reported that the Suebi were concentrating in strength and calling up reserves of horse and foot from their dependent states. I took immediate steps to secure our grain supply, chose a site for the camp, and directed the Ubii to drive their cattle and remove all their belongings from the countryside into the towns, hoping that lack of food would cause an army of inexperienced natives to fight at a grave disadvantage. The Ubii, acting on further instructions, sent frequent patrols to obtain information about the enemy's movements, and a few days later their report was handed in. Directly the Suebi had heard that a Roman army was on German soil they had moved their entire force, including allied troops, to the extreme eastern limits of their country, and had decided to await our arrival on the outskirts of an immense forest known as Bacenis, which stretched far into the interior and formed a natural barrier between themselves and the Cherusci on the middle Weser.

Political and Social Organization in Gaul and Germany

Now that we have reached this point, it may not be out of place to say a word or two about Gallic and German customs, and the characteristic differences of these two peoples. In every Gallic tribe, in every subdivision of the tribe, and almost, one might say, in every household there are rival factions controlled by men who are popularly supposed to be most influential within the group, and who therefore enjoy the last word in determining all questions of policy. This ancient practice seems to have originated in a desire to give the common folk protection against more powerful individuals. For no leader will tolerate the oppression or defrauding of his supporters: if he does, his authority is gone.

The same principle holds good for Gaul as a whole: the tribes are grouped in two factions, which at my first arrival were headed respectively by the Aedui in Burgundy and the Sequani in Franche-Comté and Alsace. The Sequani, finding their influence eclipsed by the long-standing predominance of the Aedui, whose authority extended over numerous client states, negotiated a German alliance with Ariovistus at the cost of heavy sacrifices and a promise of further concessions. A long series of victorious campaigns left them the paramount power in Gaul: the Aeduan baronage had disappeared, their satellites had transferred their allegiance, their leading men had been compelled to surrender their children as hostages and to give a solemn undertaking on behalf of their people not to intrigue against the conquerors, who then seized and occupied some Aeduan territory adjacent to their own frontier. In this extremity Divitiacus made a fruitless journey to Rome to solicit help from the Senate. But with my arrival in Gaul the situation changed: the Aedui had their hostages restored, regained their former dependencies, and even acquired some new ones as a result of my intervention. For those tribes which had lately come within the Aeduan sphere of influence enjoyed better conditions under a more equitable form of government, as well as a general improvement in their status, and a higher degree of autonomy. The hegemony had now passed from the Sequani to the Remi. As the latter were known to rank with the Aedui in our esteem, those tribes which, because of old antagonisms, could not bring themselves to accept Aeduan paramountcy, one after another committed the general direction of their policy to the Remi, who in their turn were careful to protect their interests, and thereby consolidated their own newly won and unaccustomed power. Yet, notwithstanding this hegemony, the Remi took second place in popular esteem, the Aedui being by far the most pre-eminent in that respect.

Throughout Gaul only two classes of men are of any real consequence—the Druids and the baronage. The common people are treated as little better than slaves: they never venture to act on their own initiative, and have no voice in public affairs. Most of them, burdened with debt, crushed by heavy taxation, or groaning under the hand of more powerful men, enter the service of the privileged classes, who exercise over them the rights enjoyed by a master over his slaves.

The Druids are a priestly caste. They regulate public and private sacrifices and decide religious questions. The people hold them in great respect, for they are the judges of practically all inter-tribal as well as personal disputes. They decide all criminal cases, including murder, and all disputes relating to boundaries or inheritance, awarding damages and passing sentence. Any individual or tribe refusing to abide by their decision is banned from taking part in public sacrifices—the heaviest of all their punishments. The effect of this excommunication is to set the guilty party on a level with the vilest criminals: he is shunned by all; his conversation and very presence are avoided for fear of contracting ritual uncleanness; he is barred from all honours and dignities; and he has no redress in the courts.

The Druids hold office under the supreme jurisdiction of an arch-priest who is succeeded on his death by the next senior. If there be several of equal rank, the succession is determined by the votes of their colleagues, or sometimes even by armed force. A chapter is held on a fixed date each year at a sanctuary not far from Chartres (*in finibus Carnutum*), which is reckoned the centre of Gaul; and litigants from all over the country meet there for final judgment upon their disputes.

The druidical doctrine is commonly supposed to have reached Gaul from its original home in Britain, and it is a fact that to this day men going on for higher studies usually cross to Britain for the purpose. The Druids are exempt from military service and do not pay the same taxes as the rest of the people. Such privileges attract a crowd of students, some of whom offer themselves for instruction while others are sent by their parents or relatives. It is said that these young men have to memorize endless verses, and that some of them spend as long as twenty years at their books; for although the Druids employ Greek characters for most of their secular business, such as public and private accounts, they consider it irreverent to commit their lore to writing. I suspect, however, that a double motive underlies this practice—unwillingness to publicize their teaching, and a desire to prevent students relying upon the written word at the expense of memory training; for recourse to text-books almost invariably tends to discourage learning by heart and to dull the powers of memory.

Their central dogma is the immortality and transmigration of the soul, a doctrine which they regard as the finest incentive to courage since it inspires contempt of death. But they also hold frequent discussions on astronomy, physics, and theology, in all which subjects their pupils receive instruction.

The whole baronage takes the field in the event of war —and indeed before my time these outbreaks (aggressive or defensive) might have been described as annual occurrences. Every nobleman is accompanied by his servants and armed retainers, whose greater or less number is an indication of his wealth and rank, and in fact the only recognized criterion of position and authority.

The Gallic tribes as a whole are slaves of superstition: consequently persons suffering from serious disease and those engaged in warfare or other dangerous undertakings offer, or vow to offer, human sacrifices, at which the Druids officiate. They believe that the only way to appease the divine majesty is to substitute one life for another, and regular public sacrifices are offered with the same end in view. Some of the tribes make colossal wicker-work figures, the limbs of which are filled with living men: these images are then set alight and the victims perish in a sea of flame. The gods are supposed to prefer the execution of those caught red-handed in theft, robbery with violence, or sacrilege; but if there is a shortage of these, the innocent are made to take their place.

Their principal god is Mercury, of whom there are numerous images up and down Gaul: he is regarded as inventor of all the arts; the god who points the road and guides the traveller's footsteps; the great patron of trade and riches. After Mercury come Apollo, Mars, Jupiter, and Minerva, about all of whom they have much the same ideas as other nations: Apollo averts disease, Minerva teaches the elements of industry and handicrafts, Jupiter rules the sky, Mars presides over war. Before battle the Gauls generally vow all their spoils to Mars; after victory they sacrifice the captured animals and form a pool of everything else. One sees trophies built of such material on consecrated ground in many states; and it is not often that any one dares so far ignore the claims of Heaven as to conceal the spoils of war at home or to remove them from a trophy: the crime is punishable by death under hideous torture.

The Gauls claim, on the authority of the Druids, that their whole race is descended from Dis, lord of the underworld. Accordingly they measure periods of time not by days but by nights; and in celebrating birthdays, the first of each month, and the New Year, they follow the rule that night precedes day.

One of their most distinctive social customs is the rule forbidding a child to approach his father in public until he is old enough for military service; nor is it done for a boy to stand in his father's presence when the latter goes out armed.

A husband, on marriage, adds to his wife's dowry an equivalent part of his own property: a joint account is then kept of the total, and the profits are set aside until the death of either party, when the survivor takes both shares with the accumulated profits. Husbands have the same power of life and death over their wives as over their children. When the head of a noble family dies his relatives meet, and if there is suspicion of foul play the widow is examined under torture, just as we examine slaves. If her guilt is established she is condemned to death by fire after suffering the most excruciating torments. Funerals are magnificent and expensive affairs considering the relatively low standards of life in Gaul. Everything, including even animals, that the dead man is supposed to have treasured is added to the pyre; indeed not so very long ago slaves and retainers known to have been loved by their masters were also burned with him at the conclusion of the obsequies.

A law, characteristic of the more efficient tribal constitutions, lays down that all foreign news of political importance, regardless of its source, must be reported to a magistrate, and must not be discussed with any one else. For experience has shown that unfounded reports too often breed alarm which drives ignorant and impulsive men to follow illegal courses, and to meddle in affairs that concern no one but the government. The magistrates accordingly suppress such information as they think fit, and release only what they believe good for the people to know. All political discussion is banned except in a public assembly.

The German institutions are entirely different. They have no Druids to organize religious observances and rarely indulge in sacrifice. They recognize as gods only those visible objects from which they derive obvious benefits—the Sun, for instance, the Moon, and Fire—they have never so much as heard of any others. They spend all their lives in war and the chase, and inure themselves from their earliest years to toil and hardship. Those who retain their chastity longest are held in highest honour by their fellow men; for continence, so they believe, makes a man taller, hardier, more muscular. To have had intercourse with a woman under twenty is considered the acme of disgrace; but in the matter of sex there is no prudery, men and women bathing together in the rivers, and wearing skins or short cloaks of reindeer hide which leave most of the body naked.

The Germans are not agriculturists: their principal diet is milk, cheese, and meat. They have no landed estates with definite boundaries, but the magistrates and local chiefs make an annual assignment of holdings to clans, groups of kinsmen, and other corporate bodies. The acreage and locality is at the discretion of the same authorities, and at the end of each year the assignees are compelled to move on elsewhere. The following are some of the many reasons they give for this practice: 1. To prevent the tribesmen becoming attached to one place through long association, and exchanging the military spirit for the farmer's life. 2. To control the land-grabbing instinct, and thereby to prevent dispossession of the weak by the strong. 3. To curb an immoderate desire to build houses as protection against heat and cold. 4. To discourage avarice, the root of so many factions and of so much strife. 5. To keep the masses in quiet content by letting each man see that he is as well off as his most powerful neighbour.

Every German state takes the utmost pride in devastating an area adjacent to its frontier and thereby surrounding itself with the widest possible belt of uninhabited territory. To drive one's neighbour from his land and make it too dangerous for others to settle in the vicinity is considered the essence of greatness as well as a precaution against surprise attack. On the declaration of war a high command is set up and invested with powers of life and death; but in peace-time there is no central government. Justice is administered and disputes settled by various local chiefs. Brigandage outside the tribal frontier involves no discredit: it is, rather, an acknowledged means of training the youth and an antidote to idleness. When a chieftain formally proclaims his intention of leading a raid, he calls for volunteers: those who approve the project and trust the man himself stand up and promise their support amid loud applause from the whole assembly. Any one who goes back on that promise is considered a deserter and a traitor, and no one ever trusts him again.

To harm a guest is looked upon as sacrilege. A stranger is always received in a German home, no matter why he comes: his person is sacrosanct, and he finds there a refuge and a welcome at the family board.

There was, indeed, a time when the Gauls were a more warlike race than the Germans, when they actually invaded German soil and planted colonies beyond the Rhine because their own territory was too small to support its large population. This fact explains the occupation by the Tectosagian Volcae of a district near the Hercynian Forest, which latter, I see, was known to Eratosthenes and other Greek writers as Orcynia. The invaders established permanent settlements in this most fertile part of Germany, and still enjoy a great reputation as soldiers and civil administrators.

The Germans have never risen above their ancient standards of poverty and privation; they have never so much as improved their diet and clothing. The Gauls, on the contrary, live close to the Roman Province: they have experience of seaborne trade, and are plentifully supplied with luxuries in addition to their daily requirements. Yet these same Gauls have become gradually so used to their inferiority, after numerous disasters on the field of battle, that they no longer pretend to rival the martial eminence of Germany.

The Campaign against Ambiorix

UBIAN patrols had reported a Suebic withdrawal into the forest belt, and as the Germans are not an agricultural people, there was danger of our corn supply running short. I therefore decided to advance no further and withdrew the army, taking steps, however, to remind the natives that we might yet return, and at the same time to ensure the delay of any reinforcements they might try to send into Gaul. As soon as the troops had recrossed the bridge its eastern end was broken for a distance of about two hundred feet. At the western extremity a four-storeyed tower was erected within a line of strong defence works, and left, together with the bridge, under a guard of twelve battalions commanded by a young officer, Caius Volcacius Tullus.

When the crops were beginning to ripen I set out through the forest of Ardennes for the campaign against Ambiorix. Lucius Minucius Basilus went ahead with our entire cavalry corps on the off chance that speed might enable him to strike an unexpected blow. I instructed him to forbid the lighting of camp fires, which would only serve as a long-distance signal of his approach, and told him I would follow on immediately. He carried out these instructions, completed the journey in less time than any one thought possible, and surprised many of the natives at work in their fields. Following their directions, he hurried on to a point where Ambiorix with a small cavalry escort was said to have halted.

Fortune plays a large part in warfare as in everything else: it was by sheer luck that Basilus caught the chieftain off his guard and quite unprepared; it was by sheer luck that he reached his objective before his approach was reported or even rumoured; but it was none the less by sheer luck that Ambiorix escaped with his life, though he did lose all the equipment he had with him, his horses, and his carriages. Ambiorix's house stood in a clearing like most Gallic homesteads—they generally seek the neighbourhood of woods and streams as a protection against heat. Fighting in this confined space, his friends and bodyguard managed to hold off the Roman cavalry until someone procured him a horse. The woods concealed his flight. Fortune, therefore, had led him into danger, and Fortune effected his deliverance.

But how was it that Ambiorix failed to concentrate his forces? No definite answer is possible. Was it intentional?

Had he decided against a decisive action? Or was he fore-stalled by our cavalry which he assumed would be followed shortly by the legions? What we do know is that he sent runners through the countryside with orders that every man must look after himself. Accordingly some of them took refuge in the woods, others in a continuous belt of marshland: those who lived nearest the sea hid themselves in places that were cut off from the mainland at high tide. Many left their own country altogether, and entrusted their persons and their property to complete strangers. Catuvolcus, who as king of half the Eburones had been privy to Ambiorix's scheme, was now weak with age and unable to endure the hardships of war or flight. He invoked a solemn curse upon his colleague for having suggested such a plan, and then poisoned himself with juice of the yew, a tree very common both in Gaul and Germany.

The Segni and Condrusi, two Germanic tribes whose territory lay between that of the Eburones and Treveri, sent representatives asking me not to treat them as hostile, and to discount any suggestion of a united German league west of the Rhine. They protested they had never given a thought to making war on us, and had sent Ambiorix no help. On investigation that proved true, so I told them their neutrality would be respected subject to their handing over all Eburonian fugitives at present in their dominions.

The army was now formed into three divisions, and all heavy equipment deposited in the fortress of Tongres (*Atuatucam . . . fere in mediis Eburonum finibus*), lately the winter quarters of Sabinus and Cotta. The chief of many reasons for selecting this place was that the fortifications constructed last year were still intact and would save the labour of building new ones. The depot was left in charge of the Four-teenth Legion (one of three lately recruited from Italy) and

200 cavalry, all under the command of Quintus Cicero. One division, consisting of three legions commanded by Labienus, was ordered to the Netherlands (*ad Oceanum . . . in eas partes quae Menapios attingunt*). Another three legions under Trebonius were to devastate the borders of Hesbaye (*eam regionem quae Atuatucis adiacet*), whilst I set out for the neighbourhood of Namur (*ad flumen Sabin quod influit in Mosam*), on the western edge of the Ardennes, where Ambiorix was reported to have gone with a handful of cavalry.

Before leaving Tongres I promised to return at the end of a week, in time to issue rations to the garrison. Labienus and Trebonius had orders to rejoin me there by that date if the military situation permitted, so as to collate information about the enemy's plans before resuming the campaign.

There was, as already explained, no regular native force and no stronghold with a garrison capable of opposing armed resistance: the whole population had dispersed, and each man had settled wherever some remote valley, wood, or inaccessible morass offered hope of security or defence. The natives, however, were quite familiar with these localities, and extreme care was necessary to ensure the safety of our troops. So long as they kept together they had nothing to fear from isolated bands of frightened tribesmen: the difficulty was to protect those many soldiers who were cut off one by one from the main body either because they had wandered off in search of plunder or because it was impossible for the column to proceed in close formation along overgrown and barely distinguishable forest tracks. To finish off the business and annihilate the whole pernicious gang would involve breaking up the force into numerous small detachments and sending them out on separate expeditions. On the other hand, to preserve regular company formation according to normal Roman practice would lessen our chances of damaging the enemy: it would leave them with the advantage of terrain, not to mention those individual warriors who might combine to ambush and surround any of our men who lost touch with their units. After all, the constant loss of one man here and another there can form a serious casualty list. In these difficult circumstances the most scrupulous precautions were adopted, and in spite of the troops' impatience for revenge I decided that the maximum damage we could inflict was out of all proportion to the heavy Roman losses it would undoubtedly entail. Messages were therefore sent to the surrounding tribes inviting them to enrich themselves by helping to plunder the Eburones. My real motive was to sacrifice Gallic rather than Roman lives in this dangerous forest warfare, as well as to outnumber and encircle the guilty state and to punish its crime with total annihilation. Strong forces quickly assembled from all sides, and looting began over a wide area between the Dyle and the Rhine (*in omnibus Eburonum partibus*). The week was very nearly up, and I was due back shortly at Tongres, when an incident occurred to illustrate the role of chance in military operations and its far-reaching effects. The Eburones, as we have seen, had been overawed and scattered, and there were no enemy troops in the field to cause us the least anxiety. But the Germans east of the Rhine received news of the looting and of our general invitation to take part. A force of 2,000 cavalry was hurriedly mobilized by the Sugambri, who, it may be recalled, had given asylum to the defeated Usipetes and Tencteri in their country between the Sieg and the Lippe (*qui sunt proximi Rheno*). They crossed the Rhine in boats and on rafts about twenty-eight miles below the Roman bridge (which had fortunately been left under guard); entered Eburonian territory; cut off a number of scattered fugitives; and captured large herds of cattle—a much coveted prize among these savages. Hoping for yet richer spoils, they moved further south: no marsh or forest could stop them, for they are born fighters and inveterate brigands. On inquiry as to my whereabouts they were told I had gone off on some distant expedition and that the whole Roman force had left the district. This information was supplied by prisoners, one of whom asked: 'Why go after a handful of worthless stuff when you can make a fortune in no time? In three hours,' he added, 'you can reach Tongres where the Romans have dumped all their stores. As for the garrison, it is not large enough to man the wall, and in any case none of them dare come out of the place.'

The Germans swallowed the bait: after hiding the spoils already in their possession, and guided by their informant, they made straight for Tongres.

Throughout the week following my departure Cicero obeyed his instructions and kept his men confined very closely to camp: no one, not even a servant, was allowed outside the fortress. On the seventh day, however, he began to doubt whether I would keep my appointment: there was a report that I had gone some considerable distance, but no word of my return. He was influenced, too, by complaints about his strict interpretation of orders: the men were describing their confinement as not unlike an enemy blockade. In any case, with nine legions and a strong force of cavalry to deal with an enemy who was scattered and almost non-existent, he did not envisage any grave misfortune within three miles of his camp. A reaping party of five battalions was sent out to some nearby fields, between which and the Roman fortress there stood one solitary hill. A good many legionaries on the sick list had remained in camp; about 300 of them were now convalescent, and they were sent out as a separate detachment to help with the work. Passes were also given to a crowd of servants in charge of the numerous pack-animals that we had left behind. Just at that critical moment a force of German cavalry appeared: they rode straight on without drawing rein, and tried to break in by the back gate. Some woods on that side had concealed their approach until they were quite close to the camp, so close indeed that the tradesmen, who had their booths immediately below the rampart, had no chance of escape. This unexpected attack unnerved the troops, and the battalion on guard only just managed to withstand the first onrush. The enemy swarmed round the other three sides trying to find a way in; and although the ground itself and the fortifications prevented access at other points, the troops had great difficulty in defending the gates. The whole camp was panic-stricken: the men were asking one another what it was all about, and had no idea where they were wanted or even where to fall in. Some said the place was already in enemy hands; others insisted that a victorious barbarian host had arrived after annihilating the commander-in-chief and his division. Most of them conjured up queer superstitious fancies from the very ground on which they stood, imagining they saw re-enacted the disaster that had overtaken Sabinus and Cotta, who, as they mistakenly believed, had perished in this same fortress. The Germans tried hard to force an entry, cheering, and shouting that this splendid opportunity must not be lost. For indeed the Roman panic lent colour to their prisoner's assurance that there was no effective garrison in the place.

Among the sick left behind at Tongres was Baculus, who had served under me as chief centurion of his legion, and has been referred to in connection with earlier engagements. He had lain five days unable to eat; but feeling uneasy about the legion's safety (not to mention his own), he came unarmed from his tent and saw at once that the Germans were on the point of breaking in. The situation was extremely critical; grabbing arms from the nearest soldiers, he posted himself at one of the gates and was joined by the centurions of the battalion on guard. For some time they bore the brunt of the fighting together. Baculus himself was seriously wounded: he fell unconscious, and they only just saved him by passing him back from hand to hand. This respite, however, enabled the troops to pull themselves together, to man the wall, and to make at least a show of resistance.

Meanwhile the reapers, who had by this time finished their work, heard shouting from the direction of the camp. A party of horsemen rode forward and understood the gravity of the situation. There were five battalions out there in the open, all new recruits who would be in action for the first time, with no fortifications to protect them, and completely demoralized: they stood gaping at their commanding officer and centurions, expecting to be told what to do, and the very bravest were unnerved by this emergency. The Germans now caught sight of Roman standards in the distance, and broke off their assault. At first they thought my three legions had returned from that 'distant expedition': but directly they understood how ridiculously small the force was, they attacked it from all sides. The camp servants made a dash for some rising ground close by but were quickly dislodged. They then scurried off to join various armed units, which only increased the men's terror. As the camp was so near, some of the troops proposed making a rapid charge in wedge formation: if a few were killed the rest might get through. Others were for making a united stand on the ridge and meeting their fate together. The veteran troops, who had gone out as a separate detachment, rejected the second of these plans. Led by their commander, Gaius Trebonius, a Roman knight, they charged, broke right through the enemy, and reached camp without a single loss. Following close behind them, and relying upon their magnificent effort, the servants and cavalry reached safety. Those who had chosen to make a stand on the ridge proved themselves even now hopelessly ignorant of sound tactics: they would neither stick to their original plan nor imitate the speed and drive which, as they saw, had enabled their comrades to win through. Instead they tried to get back to camp, and in order to do so came down and were trapped on low-lying ground. The centurions, some of whom had been promoted for bravery from lower grades in other legions to higher ones in the Fourteenth, were determined not to lose the reputation they had earned in previous engagements, and fell fighting with supreme courage. Their heroism forced a gap through which some of the men, much to their own surprise, reached camp. The rest were surrounded and destroyed.

When the Germans saw that the fortifications had been

manned, they abandoned hope of carrying the place by storm and retired beyond the Rhine with the loot they had concealed in the forest. Notwithstanding their departure, however, the garrison remained panic-stricken: my advance guard of cavalry under Gaius Volusenus reached camp that night, but he was unable to persuade them that I was approaching with the division intact. They were scared almost out of their wits and firmly convinced that the cavalry had merely escaped following the annihilation of three legions! Unless the whole division had been wiped out, they maintained, the Germans would never have attacked. Our arrival removed their apprehensions.

There is, of course, always an incalculable element in warfare, and I had only one complaint to make: those five battalions should never have been sent out; it was most unwise to take the slightest risk. However, the whole series of events had been largely accidental: the odds were against the sudden appearance of a hostile force, and still more heavily against its withdrawal just when the gates and rampart had been almost overwhelmed. But the strangest factor in the whole strange business was that these Germans, whose object in crossing the Rhine was to loot Ambiorix's territory, had been led quite by chance to attack the Roman camp, and had thereby rendered the Gallic chieftain as great a service as he could have possibly desired.

Our cavalry strength was now greatly increased by fresh levies from the Gallic states, and mounted units were sent out over a wide area to resume guerrilla operations. Wherever they found a village or some isolated farm they burned it and rounded up the cattle for their own use. Such crops as had not already been laid flat by the autumnal rains were gradually consumed by this huge force of men and beasts, until it seemed that any one who managed to conceal himself for the time being must inevitably die of starvation when the troops had passed.

On more than one occasion these roving detachments took prisoners who looked around in bewilderment for Ambiorix: they were sure he had been there only a few moments ago, riding for his life, and could hardly have gone far in that short time. They at once became interested, and went to quite extraordinary lengths in the hope of running the fugitive to earth and thereby winning my favour. But somehow they always just missed their quarry: Ambiorix stole away through lonely wooded glens, and made for another district under cover of darkness with an escort of four horsemen to whom alone he dared entrust his life.

After ravaging the country as described, the army (minus two whole battalions lost by Cicero) withdrew to Rheims (*Durocortorum Remorum*) where the Gallic Diet was convened, and an inquiry held into the conspiracy of the Senones and Carnutes. The ringleader, Acco, received an unusually heavy sentence, and was flogged to death in the old Roman manner. Some of the conspirators, in fear of being brought to trial, fled into exile. The legions then went into winter quarters: two in the Ardennes (*ad fines Treverorum*), two on the upper Seine (*in Lingonibus*), and the remaining six at Sens (*in Senonum finibus Agedinci*). Arrangements were made for their food supplies, and, as Gaul was now quiet, I started on my usual journey to northern Italy for the winter assizes.

BOOK SEVEN

[53 B.C.]

The Conspiracy of Vercingetorix

ON reaching Italy I heard that Publius Clodius had been assassinated and that a senatorial decree had ordered the swearing in of all able-bodied Italians of military age. I proceeded at once to enrol troops throughout the Cisalpine province. The news of these events soon reached Transalpine Gaul, where the natives not unnaturally drew their own conclusions: they invented a story that I was detained by unrest in the capital and, in view of the political situation there, could not rejoin the army. Encouraged by this opportunity of throwing off the Roman yoke that had galled them for so long, they now began quite openly to prepare for war. Their leaders met together for discussion in remote forest clearings, where they denounced the execution of Acco and reminded one another that they themselves were not immune from such a fate. They deplored the general condition of their country and offered the most splendid rewards to any one who would begin hostilities and risk his life in the cause of Gallic freedom. They agreed as a first step to devise some means of cutting me off from my troops before their scheme became too

173

widely known. That, indeed, appeared simple enough: the legions would not dare to leave winter quarters in the absence of their commander-in-chief, who in turn would find it impossible to join them without a powerful escort, which only they could supply. Anyhow, they agreed that it was better to die in battle than to forgo in perpetuity their ancient military renown and their ancestral liberty.

After these preliminary negotiations, a plenary session was held, at which the Carnutes accepted responsibility on behalf of the states, and undertook to strike the first blow. An exchange of hostages at this juncture might reveal their intentions, and the Carnutes therefore demanded an oath in presence of the assembled war standards (one of the most solemn of Gallic rites), whereby the parties swore not to desert the cause once hostilities had begun. The assembly rose to the Carnutian envoys; all present took the oath, a date was agreed for the revolt, and the representatives dispersed.

On the appointed day the Carnutes, led by two bandits, Cotuatus and Conconnetodumnus, made a sudden swoop on Orleans, massacred the Roman population (business men who had settled in the town), and plundered their property Among the victims was Gaius Fufius Cita, a respectable Roman knight whom I had put in charge of the grain supply. The tidings swept through Gaul; for whenever anything particularly interesting or important occurs the news is passed by word of mouth, from one individual to another, right across country. On this occasion the massacre of Orleans, which had taken place at about 8 a.m., was known in Auvergne, just over 150 miles away, some twelve hours later.

Here the conflagration took a rapid hold, inspired by Vercingetorix, a young Arvernian who wielded enormous influence. His father, Celtillus, had exercised a kind of general jurisdiction over the whole of Gaul, but had been murdered by his immediate subjects for attempting to make himself absolute ruler. Vercingetorix mobilized his retainers and was quickly joined by others as soon as his purpose became known. Some of the chiefs, including his uncle Gobbanitio, tried to dissuade him on the grounds that his enterprise was far too risky. Driven from Gergovia he did not lose heart, but went through the countryside gathering a band of beggars and outcasts. Thenceforward he succeeded in winning over every Arvernian he met: calling upon them to take arms in defence of Gallic liberty, he soon mustered a powerful force, and expelled his opponents in their turn. He was now proclaimed king by his followers, and sent ambassadors all over the country urging the tribes to stand by him in the approaching conflict. Before long he had won support in districts as far apart as Sens, Paris, Poitiers, Cahors, Tours, Évreux, Limoges, Angers (*Senones, Parisios, Pictones, Cadurcos, Turanos, Aulercos, Lemovices, Andes*), and the whole Atlantic seaboard.

Armed with this power, he demanded hostages from all his allied states; ordered each of them to furnish a specified number of troops without delay; and gave directions for the manufacture of a fixed quota of arms by a certain date, with special attention to cavalry requirements. Thorough in everything, he backed his authority with a savage discipline that would tolerate no wavering: more serious cases were punished with torture and the stake, while those guilty in a less degree were sent home without their ears, or perhaps with one eye gouged out, to serve as a warning to others of the stern penalties a delinquent might expect.

This terrorism resulted before long in the assembly of a regular army. Part of it was sent to Le Rauergne (*in Rutenos*) under a dashing Cadurcan officer named Lucterius, while Vercingetorix himself started for Berry (*in Bituriges*).

175

On his approach the Bituriges sent envoys to the Aedui, whose suzerainty they acknowledged, asking for help to strengthen their defences. Acting on advice from the generals whom I had left in charge of the Roman army, the Aeduan Government dispatched reinforcements of both infantry and cavalry; but when these reached the Loire, which marks the boundary between the two tribes, they halted, and returned after a few days without venturing across the river. They explained to the Roman staff that they were afraid of treachery, for there was reliable information that the Bituriges and Arverni had agreed to cut them off on both sides if once they crossed the Loire. Whether this was the true reason I do not know, and therefore abstain from any positive assertion. It may have been due to their own disaffection: at any rate, as soon as they withdrew, the Bituriges went over to the rebels.

News of these events reached me in Italy. I was informed that the situation at Rome was less explosive, thanks to firm handling by Pompey, and I therefore left immediately for Transalpine Gaul. Once there I was faced with a very difficult problem: how to rejoin the legions. If they were summoned to the Province they would clearly have to fight a pitched battle *en route* without their commander-in-chief; and as for making the journey myself, none of the tribes could be trusted, no matter how quiet they seemed.

Meanwhile, however, Lucterius had begun his mission and won over the Ruteni. He then marched into Agennois and the Gévandau (*in Nitiobroges et Gabalos*), where he took hostages from the Nitiobroges and Gabali, and raised a strong force with which he then hurried south. His objective was the Roman Province in the area of Narbonne. This emergency demanded the postponement of all other business. I went straight to Narbonne, reassured the frightened inhabitants, and stationed detachments of the provincial garrison around the city as well as at various danger points on a line between Nîmes and Toulouse (*in Rutenis provincialibus, Volcis Arecomecis, Tolosatibus*). Lucterius was thereby checked and forced to retire: he thought it too risky to attempt infiltration through our positions. I therefore set out for the Vivarais (*in Helvios*) where the rest of the garrison and a fresh draft of recruits from Italy had been ordered to concentrate.

It was now midwinter: snow lay thick on the Cévennes which separate that district from Auvergne, and all passes were blocked. Yet my troops accomplished the prodigious feat of cutting a road through drifts up to 6 feet deep, and thereby enabled us to get through. The Arverni were taken by surprise: they believed the Cévennes as good a fortification as any wall; at that time of year, in fact, the range was considered impassable even for single travellers. The Roman cavalry was ordered to ride through the country and do their best to terrorize the population; and it was not long before rumour, followed quickly by official dispatches, informed Vercingetorix of these events. The natives were seriously alarmed: they pestered him to consider their safety and protect them from these raids, especially as they had now to bear the brunt of the campaign. He gave way to their entreaties, and removed his camp from Berry to Auvergne. That was just what I expected, so two days later I left the army under the command of young Brutus with instructions to continue cavalry operations over the widest possible area. The ostensible reason of my journey was to raise fresh levies and some cavalry reinforcements, but, much to the surprise of my attendants, we travelled at full speed to Vienne. There I picked up a fresh escort and then rode day and night up the Saône valley into Burgundy (*per fines Haeduorum in Lingones*), where two of the legions had their winter quarters. The purpose of all this hurry was to forestall any design which the Aedui might entertain against my life.

Arrived in Burgundy, I summoned the other legions and had them concentrated before the Arverni heard the news, but directly Vercingetorix received intelligence of this move he once again marched through Berry and laid siege to the fortress of Gorgobina, which had been established as a Boian settlement under Aeduan suzerainty after the defeat of the Helvetii.

A day's march brought us to Montargis (*Vellaunodunum*), to which I laid siege so as not to endanger the supply route by leaving an enemy hanging on my rear. Lines of contravallation were thrown up within forty-eight hours, and on the third day envoys came out to negotiate terms of surrender. They were directed to stack their arms, hand over their live-stock, and deliver 600 hostages. Being anxious to reach my principal objective in the shortest possible time, I left Trebonius to supervise the execution of these orders while the main column pushed on to Orleans (*Cenabum*). The Carnutes had only just been notified that Montargis was invested: they imagined it would be a long drawn-out affair, and were assembling troops for the defence of Orleans when we arrived before that city at the end of a two days' march. By the time camp was pitched the day was too far advanced to warrant an immediate attack, but I gave orders for preparations to be made for an assault on the following day. As there was a bridge leading directly from the town over the Loire, two legions were detailed to remain on guard all night and to prevent a possible escape under cover of darkness. Sure enough, the citizens moved silently out of the town a little after midnight

and began to cross the river. When our patrols brought word of this I had the gates fired and sent in the two legions on duty. They took possession of the place, and all but a mere handful of its inhabitants were made prisoner; for the streets and bridge were too narrow to allow the passage of that great crowd of fugitives. Orleans was sacked, the loot was distributed among the soldiers, and we crossed the Loire into Berry (*in Biturigum fines*).

When the news reached Ver-cingetorix, he raised the siege of Gorgobina and hurried to meet us. We had already invested Neuvy (*Noviodunum*), a strong-hold on our route, when a de-putation arrived begging me to pardon the city and spare the lives of its population. Not wish-ing to interrupt the quick succes-sion of victories that had so far favoured us, I imposed the same terms as at Montargis. Some of the hostages had already been surrendered, and a party of centurions had taken a few troops into the town to collect arms and live-stock, when Vercin-getorix's advance guard of cavalry appeared. Immediately the townsfolk caught sight of it they decided there was a chance of relief: they raised a tremendous yell, rushed to arms, closed their gates, and proceeded to man the wall.

The centurions inside the town, realizing that all this ex-citement meant fresh trouble, mounted guard on the gates with drawn swords and got their men safely away. Our cavalry went out to engage the Gallic horse; they found themselves in difficulty, but were reinforced by a party of some 400 German troopers which had been attached to the army from the start of this campaign. The German charge was irresistible, and the enemy fell back with heavy casualties. The inhabitants were again demoralized by this reverse, and seizing the reputed leaders of the sedition, they turned them over to me and surrendered.

Siege of Bourges

FOLLOWING the capitulation of Neuvy I moved against Bourges (*Avaricum*), the largest and strongest Biturigan town, lying in the most fertile district of Berry; for it seemed probable that the reduction of this place would compel the whole tribe to submit. Having experienced three successive defeats, at Montargis, Orleans, and Neuvy, Vercingetorix held a council of war and advocated a complete revision of the Gallic plans. Their first endeavour, he said, must be to deprive the Romans of forage and other supplies—an easy matter, considering the Gauls were strong in cavalry and also had the season in their favour: there was no grass to cut, so the enemy would have to disperse over the countryside to get hay from the farms, and these small isolated parties could be mopped up one by one. Second, all rights of private ownership must be sacrificed in the common interest: villages and farms must be burned everywhere along the Roman line of march, and on each side of it as far as their foragers could possibly reach. The Gauls, he added, were abundantly supplied with such necessities, and could draw on the resources of the local tribes. The Romans, on the other hand, were faced with sure starvation, which they could avoid only by going dangerously far from camp in search of food, and it would then be immaterial whether they were killed outright or simply deprived of their transport, the loss of which must, in any case, render their campaign impossible. Finally, all towns would have to be burned unless they were clearly impregnable on account of their natural strength or their fortifications.

These measures, he acknowledged, might be thought unfair and even terribly cruel; but he urged his hearers to remember that the alternative was infinitely worse: slavery for their wives and children, death for themselves—the universal fate of conquered peoples.

The council were unanimous in adopting Vercingetorix's plan; and more than twenty Biturigan cities were delivered to the flames in a single day. The Gauls watched this holocaust with heavy hearts, but consoled themselves with the belief that victory was now assured and that their losses would be very soon made good. A general assembly discussed the fate of Bourges: the Biturigan delegates went down on their knees before the representatives of each tribe in turn, and implored them not to insist upon the destruction by its own citizens of one of the fairest towns in Gaul, the main bulwark and the glory of their state. They assured the assembly that its natural strength made the place easy to defend, for it was almost entirely surrounded by streams and marshland, through which one narrow opening alone gave access. Their request was granted, and though Vercingetorix at first opposed it, he afterwards yielded at the instance of the Bituriges whose petition had, indeed, won general support.

The Gallic commander now followed us by easy stages and chose for the site of his camp a spot protected by marsh and forest, just over fifteen miles from Bourges. He kept himself informed of events inside the town by means of patrols at regular intervals throughout the day, and was constantly on the watch for our troops going out in search of fodder or corn. They were obliged to wander far afield, and by attacking them in isolated groups he inflicted serious losses, notwithstanding every effort on our part to counter-act his measures by leaving at irregular hours and by dif-ferent routes.

The Roman camp stood on that side of the town where there was a narrow gap in the surrounding marshland and watercourses. As the terrain made contravallation impractic-able, our first move was the construction, under cover of mantlets, of a siege terrace with a tower at either end. Meanwhile I was pressing the Boii and Aedui for grain. The latter were only half-hearted and gave little help, while the Boii, a small unimportant tribe, needed what they had for home consumption. All neighbouring granaries had been burned, and the troops found themselves in the dangerous predicament of being for several days without grain. They only managed to avoid starvation by driving in cattle from distant villages; but not one of them was heard to utter a single word that might be considered unworthy of Rome and her victorious arms. Indeed when I spoke to the men of each legion at their work, and told them I was ready to call off the siege if they found their privations unbearable, they were unanimous in asking me not to do so. The bat-talion commanders and centurions brought me a message from the men, which stated that, having served under me for so long without suffering the humiliation of an un-finished task, they would feel themselves disgraced if the siege were abandoned: they preferred any hardship to failure in avenging the massacre of Orleans.

Our terrace had progressed and the siege-towers were already close to the wall, when some prisoners informed us that Vercingetorix had run short of forage and had

moved his camp nearer the city. He himself had taken a
detachment of cavalry and some light infantry, who
regularly accompanied them in battle, to ambush a place
where he expected our foragers would go next day. We
started at midnight and reached the Gallic camp in the early
hours, but their patrols had given the alarm: they had
hidden their carts and equipment deep in the woods and
formed up in strength on an open ridge. The troops were
immediately given orders to stack packs and prepare for
action.

The ground occupied by the enemy formed a gradual
slope, but was almost surrounded on the level by a marsh
that was virtually impassable, though no more than 50
feet wide. The natives had broken down the causeways over
this marsh, and relying on the strength of their position,
stood firm on the ridge. They were formed up by tribes,
and covered every means of approach from thickets which
bordered the morass: they intended, if we tried forcing our
way across, to charge downhill on the legions as they
floundered in the mud. Seeing how close together the two
forces were, one would have said the Gauls meant business
and that chances were even: but any one who observed the
disparity of fighting conditions would have recognized their
defiance as mere bravado. Our fellows were maddened by
the audacity of an enemy who stood watching them at
that close range. They clamoured for the signal to attack,
but I explained that victory on this occasion could be won
only at enormous cost. 'Hundreds of brave men,' I said,
'will inevitably die. I know you are ready to face any danger
at my command; but for that very reason I should be guilty
of damnable injustice if I put my reputation before your
lives.' They saw the point; we returned to camp and carried on with siege operations.

When Vercingetorix returned he was accused of treachery on the grounds that he had moved his camp nearer the Roman position, and had then gone off with his entire cavalry strength, leaving a large army with no commander and the enemy with a heaven-sent opportunity. All this, they insisted, could not have been accidental; it must have been carefully planned. They also charged him with pre-ferring to hold the Gallic kingdom by Roman favour than as a gift from his own people.

In reply to their accusations Vercingetorix reminded them that he had moved camp at their own request because they were short of forage. In occupying a site that was admitted-ly somewhat close to the enemy, he had considered only the advantage of a position whose natural strength alone was sufficient for its defence. Again, there could have been no need of cavalry on marshy ground, whereas it had proved most useful elsewhere. He had intentionally abstained from appointing a deputy commander, who might have been driven by popular outcry to fight a general engagement, which every one seemed to want, as they were soft and unequal to prolonged exertion. If the enemy's arrival, he continued, was fortuitous, Fortune alone was to blame; if it was the result of information given by a traitor they had the traitor to thank for providing them with a bird's-eye view of the enemy's small numbers and for showing them the wretched spirit of an army that slunk back to camp without showing fight. As for the royal title, he had no wish to obtain it from a Roman general as the price of treachery when he could, and most certainly would, merit it on the field of battle at the head of his Gauls. They could keep their titles if they regarded a crown as the symbol of his personal honour rather than as the pledge of their final victory. 'To satisfy yourselves,' he cried, 'that I speak the truth, listen to what these Roman soldiers have to say!' Thereupon he introduced a number of our camp servants: they had been caught when foraging some days earlier, and after being tortured with starvation in chains had been carefully primed with the answers they were to give when questioned. These men obediently stated that they were legionaries, and had been driven by hunger and want to steal out of camp in hope of finding some corn or cattle in the fields. The whole Roman army, they said, was in the same plight: the physical strength of the troops was at a very low ebb; they were quite unfit for work, and the commander-in-chief had decided to abandon the siege and retire in three days' time unless some progress had been made.

'That,' exclaimed Vercingetorix, 'is what you owe me whom you now accuse of treason! As a result of my fore-sight this great and victorious army is nearly destroyed by famine without your shedding a drop of blood; and I have also taken steps to ensure that when it suffers the final ignominy of a disorderly retreat no tribe will allow it to cross their frontier.'

The whole assembly cheered and clashed their shields— the usual Gallic method of approving a speech. Vercinget-orix was declared a first-rate leader and a brilliant strategist whose loyalty was beyond question. It was also decided to send 10,000 picked troops into the city and not to entrust the defence solely to the Bituriges who, if they managed to save the town, would claim the victory as exclusively their own.

The matchless courage of our troops was opposed with every sort of contrivance; for the Gauls are a most ingenious race, quick to borrow and develop any idea suggested to them by others. They caught our siege-hooks in nooses

185

and hauled them inside by means of windlasses. They also tried undermining the terrace, a job to which they brought all the skill acquired by long experience in the great iron mines of Gaul.

The normal pattern of a Gallic town wall is as follows. Balks of timber are laid at regular intervals of 2 feet along the ground plan and at right angles to it. These are mortised on the inside and covered with a good thickness of rubble, the spaces between each balk being filled on the outer side with large stones. When the first course is complete, another is added on top: the same interval is kept between the balks of this second course; but no two courses are in direct contact, being separated by layers of stone 2 feet high which bind each tier of balks and rubble firmly together. In this way the wall is raised stage by stage to the required height; and the finished structure is by no means unsightly, presenting a variegated surface of alternate balks and stones, each in its own straight line. It is also a most serviceable piece of defensive work: the masonry is fire-proof, and the timber quite impervious to a battering-ram which can neither pierce nor shatter a framework mortised on the inside with 40-feet beams.

The garrison of Bourges had mounted along the whole circuit of their wall a superstructure of wooden turrets covered with hides. In frequent day and night sorties they tried setting fire to our terrace and attacking the men at work upon it. As the increasing height of the terrace raised the towers a little more each day, the Gauls added to their own turrets by laying floors between the projecting up-rights of the framework. They also counter-mined our sub-terranean galleries, and prevented their extension to the wall by driving in fire-hardened stakes or throwing in molten pitch and enormous stones.

These measures, added to the cold and ceaseless rain, made operations extraordinarily difficult; but all such obstacles were overcome by the relentless effort of our troops, who in twenty-five days completed a terrace 319 feet long and just over 77 feet high. I used regularly to stay up at night with the men to see that work was not interrupted; and on one such occasion, a little before midnight, smoke was observed rising from the terrace, which by then almost touched the wall. The enemy had undermined and set it on fire. At the same moment we heard cheering all along the wall, and some of the defenders made a rush from two gates on either side of our towers: others flung torches and dry wood, or poured down pitch and other inflammable material on to the terrace. It was hard to know where first to meet this attack, and at what points help was required. However, I had made a practice of keeping two legions on night duty before the camp while larger numbers were engaged on the works, and the situation was quickly in hand: some went to hold the attacking force, others pulled back the towers and made a gap in the terrace, while the troops in camp ran out to extinguish the flames.

Fighting continued at all points for the rest of that night; and the enemy's hope of success was constantly renewed, especially when they saw that the screens protecting our towers were burned. Our troops had no cover, and so found difficulty in moving up to help their comrades. The defenders, on the other hand, continually sent fresh men to relieve those who were exhausted: they were convinced that the fate of Gaul hung upon these critical hours, and we now witnessed an episode which I feel should be noticed here.

There was a Gaul standing just outside one of the gates, receiving lumps of tallow and pitch that were passed along to him, and hurling them into the flames opposite one of

our towers. This man was mortally wounded in the right
side by a shot from a quick-firing catapult. One of his
comrades stepped over his prostrate body and carried on
with his job. He was likewise shot dead; a third took his

place, then a fourth, and so on. The post was only abandoned when the fire had been extinguished and the enemy
thrown back at all points.

The Gauls had now tried every expedient without success, and next day they decided to obey an urgent summons from Vercingetorix to evacuate the town. They hoped
that by making this attempt at dead of night they might
get through without serious loss, as Vercingetorix's camp
was not far away, and the continuous belt of marshland
that lay around the city would hinder our pursuit. Darkness had fallen, and they were preparing to carry out their
plan, when the married women suddenly ran into the streets
and knelt before their husbands, begging not to be left
with their children to the tender mercies of the enemy
simply because they had not the physical strength to join
the exodus. But extreme danger has little room for pity;
and when these ladies realized that their menfolk were

adamant they began screaming and making signs to our troops who were thereby warned of the impending flight. The Gauls were alarmed by this turn of events; they were afraid our cavalry would forestall them on the roads, and therefore abandoned the whole scheme.

Next day we completed the terrace and moved forward one of the towers. It began to rain heavily, and this seemed the moment to attempt an assault, especially as the guards on the wall had been rather carelessly posted. The troops were therefore directed to go haphazardly about their work, and the officers received their final briefing. While the legions prepared for action under cover of mantlets, an order of the day told them the hour had come to avenge themselves for all their labour, and announced prizes for the first men on the wall. I then gave the signal to attack. They rushed suddenly from cover all along the line, and were soon crowding on the wall. The garrison was taken by surprise and panicked: they were driven from the defences, but regrouped in wedge formation on the market square and other open places, determined to make an orderly stand against attack from wherever it came. However, when they saw the legions pouring round the entire circuit without a single man coming down to meet them, they were terrified at the prospect of being cut off from all chance of escape. They threw away their arms, and ran for their lives to the farthest quarter of the town. There some were cut down by the legions as they jammed the narrow gateways; others managed to get out, but were slaughtered by the cavalry. None of our troops gave a moment's thought to plunder: they were so infuriated by the massacre of Orleans and the labour of this siege, that they spared neither the aged nor women nor children. Indeed from a total population of some 40,000, a bare 800,

who had fled at the first alarm, got through to Vercingetorix. He intercepted them late at night, being afraid that
if they entered camp in a body they might arouse such pity
among the rank and file of his army that a general mutiny
would follow. His personal friends and the tribal chiefs
were stationed at some distance along the road with orders
to sort out the fugitives and take them to their respective
tribes in various parts of the camp which had been assigned
to each at the start of the campaign.

Next day Vercingetorix held a conference: he expressed
his sympathy with the victims of this latest reverse, but insisted that they must not be unduly worried or upset. The
Romans, he said, had not won by courage in the open
field, but by cunning and expert knowledge of siege craft,
with which the Gauls had not much acquaintance. It was,
in any case, foolish to expect unvarying success in war: his
hearers could bear witness that he had never really liked
the idea of defending Bourges, and this set-back was due
to their having lent unreasoning support to an impractic-
able scheme of the Bituriges. However, he promised before
long to repair the damage with yet greater victories: he
was, he said, doing his utmost to win over the tribes that
had so far held aloof, and once a really united Gallic league
was formed the whole world could not stand against it.
Such a league, he assured them, was already on the way to
becoming a reality: in the meantime it was only fair that
they should take measures to protect themselves by fortify-
ing the camp, so as more easily to resist a sudden attack.

His speech was received with enthusiasm: it was particularly gratifying to realize that their commander had not
lost heart and had faced them boldly instead of hiding himself away in shame. He was now thought to possess extraordinary foresight and prudence in having, while there was

still time, counselled first the destruction of Bourges and later its evacuation. The authority of a commander is generally weakened by failure: Vercingetorix's reputation, on the contrary, was enhanced with every day that followed this defeat. Their hopes were raised by his assurance that other tribes could be won over to the cause, and for the first time in Gallic history a native army proceeded to fortify its camp: though quite unused to such labour, they had suffered a terrible blow and felt they must submit to anything demanded of them. Vercingetorix was as good as his word, and worked strenuously to bring in the tribes still outside the alliance. He tried to enlist the favour of their chieftains by gifts and the promise of rewards. His agents were either personal friends of the chiefs or men selected for their powers of subtle argument: all were highly qualified for the job they had to do. He also provided arms and clothing for the refugees from Bourges; and, in order to bring his army once more up to strength, he ordered each tribe to supply a certain number of troops who were to present themselves at his headquarters by a given date. Finally he ordered a census of the numerous Gallic archers, who were to be conscripted and sent to join him. By these means the losses sustained at Bourges were made good, and while his instructions were being carried out he was reinforced by King Teutomatus of the Nitiobroges, who came with a strong body of cavalry made up of his own subjects and some Aquitanian mercenaries. Teutomatus was the son of Ollovico who had been styled 'Friend' by the senate.

We delayed for some days at Bourges: huge stocks of grain and other provisions were found there, and enabled the troops to recover from fatigue and under-nourishment. Winter was now almost over, and I had decided to resume the campaign in early spring: my plan was to entice the enemy from the marshland and forest regions, or else to reduce them by blockade. At this juncture a mission of Aeduan chiefs arrived at headquarters to ask my help in a matter of the utmost importance. The situation, they said, was critical: according to long-established custom they elected a single magistrate to hold sovereign power for one year, but there were at present two such magistrates in office, each claiming that he alone had been constitutionally appointed. One was Convictolitavis, a distinguished young aristocrat; the other was Cotus, the scion of a very ancient family, a man of great personal influence and important family connections, whose brother Valetiacus had held the same office a year ago. The whole country was armed to the teeth; both council and people were divided, and each claimant had his own following. If the quarrel went a stage further civil war was inevitable, and it seemed that the only way of preventing that was for me to exert my authority without delay.

It was unfortunate to have to interrupt military operations; but, knowing the disastrous consequences which too often arise from such disputes, I decided that my first duty was to prevent a clash which would inevitably result in an appeal to Vercingetorix by the weaker party. The Aedui were a powerful tribe, bound by the closest ties to Rome, and the constant recipients of my favour and support: their constitution forbade the chief magistrate to leave his country, and, in order to avoid any appearance of contempt for Aeduan law, I decided to go there in person. The whole tribal council and the rival claimants were instructed to meet me at Décize (*Decetia*), where the conference was attended by nearly all members of the government. I was informed that Valetiacus had announced his brother's appointment in a small private gathering summoned at an irregular time and place; this had been done, moreover, in violation of a statute which forbade two members of one family to hold office, or even a seat on the council, during the lifetime of both. I therefore directed Cotus to resign and confirmed the election of Convictolitavis, which had been held when the office was vacant, was constitutional in form, and approved by the Druids. After making this award I advised the Aedui to forget their differences, to concentrate exclusively on the war, and to rely upon me to repay their services when the conquest of Gaul was completed. I also ordered them to send me all their cavalry and 10,000 infantry for escort duty on our various supply routes.

Gergovia, 52 B.C.

THE army was now formed into two divisions: Labienus marched with four legions to Senonois and the Île de France, (*in Senones Parisiosque*), whilst I took the other six up the Allier valley towards Gergovia in Auvergne. The cavalry was divided proportionately between our two forces. On learning this, Vercingetorix had all bridges over the Allier destroyed and began his march along the other bank. The two armies were in sight of one another, and the Gauls generally encamped directly opposite to us, patrolling the bank to prevent our bridging the river. The situation was most awkward: it seemed that the Allier would remain an obstruction for the rest of that summer, as it cannot usually be forded before autumn. To resolve this difficulty we pitched camp one evening in a wooded area opposite to where Vercingetorix had had one of the native bridges destroyed. Next day I kept two legions hidden there and sent on the remainder with all our heavy equipment: they were in normal column of route (except that some battalions were broken up into smaller units so as to make it appear that all six legions were on the road), and had orders to advance as far as possible. After allowing them time for a full day's march we began rebuilding the bridge on its original piles, the lower parts of which remained intact. That was soon done: the legions crossed and chose a site for their camp, and the remainder of my force was recalled. Vercingetorix now began pushing quickly ahead, anxious to avoid a pitched battle until he considered the moment opportune; and five days later we reached Gergovia, where a cavalry skirmish was fought on the same day.

The next step was a reconnaissance of the town. As it stood on a very lofty eminence and was difficult of access on all sides I gave up the idea of taking it by assault, but decided not to begin siege operations before securing our food supplies. Vercingetorix had encamped near the city with the tribal contingents posted at short intervals round his headquarters. Occupying the whole ridge within view between Gergovia and the heights of Risolles to the south-west (*omnibus eius iugi collibus*), they presented a formidable appearance. Every morning at dawn he summoned a meeting of his staff to co-ordinate intelligence and to deal with routine business. On most days, too, he sent cavalry into action with archers among their ranks in order to exercise the skill and courage of his men.

Opposite the town, and projecting from the southern slope of Gergovia, was the Roche Blanche (*collis*), a very steep hill of great natural strength: once in possession of it, we should clearly be able to deprive the enemy of his main water supply and to restrict the movement of his foragers. Although the position was held by a fairly strong Gallic detachment, we left camp at dead of night, dislodged them, and captured the height. Two legions were stationed there in a small camp connected with our main base by two parallel trenches, each about six feet wide, which enabled the men to pass to and fro, even singly, without fear of sudden attack.

During these preliminary operations before Gergovia the newly appointed Aeduan Vergobret, Convictolitavis, having been bribed by the Arverni, opened negotiations with Litaviccus and his brothers, who were members of an aristocratic family and leaders of a gang of youths. He shared his bribe with them, and reminded them that they were freeborn men destined to rule. The Aedui alone, he explained, stood in the way of an otherwise certain Gallic victory: they alone kept other tribes loyal to Rome, who would have no chance in Gaul without them. He agreed that he was to some extent in my debt, but argued that I had merely adjudicated on a cast-iron case, and that national liberty must be his first consideration. There was no more reason, he said, why Rome should be called on to decide native rights and interpret native laws than that they should be invited to sit as judges in the Roman courts. The young men were quickly won over by the Vergobret's eloquence, not to mention his gold, and promised to take the lead in this enterprise. But the first question was how to set about it; for they were not at all sure that the people could be induced offhand to shoulder the responsibility of war. It was eventually decided that Litaviccus should take command of the 10,000 troops who were going to reinforce the Roman army, while his brothers hurried on ahead to join me at Gergovia. The scheme was then worked out in detail.

Litaviccus took over his command, and had reached a point some twenty-eight miles from his destination when he suddenly halted, paraded his troops, and addressed them in tears: 'Soldiers, where are we going? All our cavalry, the flower of our manhood, have perished. Two of our leading citizens, Eporedorix and Viridomarus, have been accused of treason by the Romans and executed without a trial. All my brothers and other relations have been murdered; I cannot bring myself to describe to you what exactly happened, but listen to these fellows who escaped from the massacre.' He then produced some men who had been carefully primed to fill in his story. They told how the entire Aeduan cavalry force had been butchered for an alleged intrigue with the Arverni, and how they themselves had escaped by mixing with the troops while the massacre was in progress. The whole mob began yelling with rage, and implored Litaviccus to do something for them. 'There's no question about it,' he replied, 'we must march straight to Gergovia and link up with the Arverni. You can bet your lives the Romans are already following up this atrocious crime and hurrying to deal with us likewise. If we've any guts left, let's avenge the foul murder of our people on these ruffians!' Here he pointed to some Roman citizens who were travelling with him in reliance on his protection. They were immediately seized, tortured to death, and the large stores of grain they carried with them ransacked. Litaviccus then sent couriers through the Aeduan countryside to rouse the population with the same lies about a massacre of their cavalry and chieftains, and called on them to avenge themselves in the same fashion as he had done.

Now I had personally summoned Eporedorix and Viridomarus to serve with our Gallic horse. The former was a young nobleman with a good deal of influence among his people. Viridomarus was of about the same age and equally popular; he was not of noble birth, but I had raised him, on Divitiacus's recommendation, from humble circumstances to the highest honours. The two were rivals for power, and in the recent dispute over the magistracy Eporedorix had been an active supporter of Convictolitavis, Viridomarus of Cotus. One night, about twelve o'clock, Eporedorix came and told me of Litaviccus's design, of which he had just received information: he begged me not to allow the tribe to throw off its allegiance at the prompting of these young hooligans, as would assuredly happen if Vercingetorix were reinforced by 10,000 Aeduan troops, to whose fate neither their relations nor their government could remain indifferent.

This was grave news, for I had always shown the Aedui special favour and allowed them special privileges. Without a moment's delay I started with all my cavalry and four legions in light marching order. At such crisis, when everything depended on speed, there was no time to reduce the area of the camp, and two legions under Fabius were left to guard it as well as the smaller camp at Roche Blanche. I ordered the arrest of Litaviccus's brothers, but discovered they had fled to the enemy an hour or so earlier. An order of the day warned the troops that the present emergency necessitated a long fatiguing march, and there must be no grumbling. The response from all ranks was magnificent, and a journey of twenty-three miles brought us in sight of the enemy column. Our cavalry rode forward and effectively halted its advance, but they had orders to kill no one, while Eporedorix and Viridomarus, who were supposed to be dead, moved through the lines of horsemen and spoke to their countrymen. As soon as they were recognized and Litaviccus's deceit understood, the Aedui stretched out their hands in token of surrender, threw down their arms, and begged for their lives. Litaviccus himself escaped to Gergovia with his retainers, who, according to Gallic custom, might not desert their lord in the most desperate situation.

Notice was sent to the Aeduan authorities of a free pardon granted to the rebels. They might have been put to death in accordance with the rules of war.

My troops were allowed a three hours' rest before starting back for Gergovia, and we had covered about half the distance when some horsemen rode up with news of a dangerous situation at the camp. The enemy, it appeared, had attacked in strength, throwing in wave after wave of fresh troops: the defence had been almost exhausted because the size of the camp required every man at his post on the rampart, and made it impossible to keep troops in reserve. Our artillery had proved invaluable, but we had suffered heavy casualties under a hail of arrows and other missiles. The Gauls had eventually retired, and Fabius was now engaged barricading all but two of the gates and adding breastworks to the rampart in preparation for a similar attack next day. On the strength of this report my soldiers made a tremendous effort and reached camp before sunrise.

Meanwhile, however, the Aedui received Litaviccus's first dispatch. They took no trouble to verify its contents, but allowed themselves to be driven by greed, anger, or mere impetuosity (the Gallic temperament again!) into accepting idle rumour as established fact. Roman citizens were murdered or enslaved, their property looted; and Convictolitavis added to the confusion by rousing the mob to frenzy, in the hope that if a really serious outrage were committed shame would prevent their return to reason. Marcus Aristius, a Roman battalion commander, had stopped at Chalon-sur-Saône (*Cavillonum*) on the way to rejoin his legion: he was ordered out of the town, together with some Roman merchants who lived there, and given a safe conduct: but no sooner had they started than the inhabitants set upon them, stole their luggage, and, because they resisted, kept up the attack for a whole day and night. Many had been killed on both sides, and a still larger crowd had collected, when news arrived that the whole Aeduan contingent had been trapped and was at my mercy. The town council hurried to Aristius and assured him that they had had no part in this unfortunate incident. They ordered an inquiry into the theft of Roman goods, confiscated the property of Litaviccus and his brothers, and sent a deputation to my headquarters to make excuses. Their real object was to secure the release of their troops; for, much as they dreaded retribution for their crimes, they were equally fascinated by the profits to be made out of loot, and had already begun secret preparations for war by sending envoys to invite the support of other tribes.

All this was perfectly clear to me; but I replied to their envoys in the mildest possible terms, and told them that notwithstanding the irresponsible shortsightedness of the common people my regard for the Aeduan state was undiminished, and they would not be judged too harshly. The fact was, I anticipated a more serious Gallic rising, and in order to avoid encirclement by a ring of hostile tribes I was beginning to think of withdrawing from Gergovia and regrouping the whole army. It was important, however, that our departure should not resemble headlong flight inspired by fear of more widespread rebellion, and the problem was still uppermost in my mind when I thought I saw an opportunity to strike a decisive blow.

On going to inspect defence works at Roche Blanche (*minora castra*), I noticed that one of the Risolles heights (*collem*) within the Gallic lines was completely deserted. Until now it had been held by the enemy in such strength that the ground was scarcely visible. This was strange, and

I questioned some of the many deserters who were reaching our camp every day. They unanimously confirmed information we had already obtained through our patrols: the crest of the Risolles (*dorsum . . . eius iugi*) was almost level, but narrow and wooded at the Col des Goules (*qua esset aditus ad alteram partem oppidi*) which adjoined the southwestern corner of the town. The Gauls, they said, were most anxious about the security of this point, and were sure that if they lost a second height in addition to Roche Blanche (*uno colle ab Romanis occupato si alterum amisissent*) they would be fairly cut off and unable to reach the town or to send out foraging parties. Vercingetorix had therefore recalled every available man to defend the Col des Goules (*hunc locum*).

Just after midnight I sent out several parties of horse with instructions to ride through the district with rather more noise than usual. At daybreak a long train of pack-horses and mules was unharnessed and led out: the drivers, wearing helmets to look like cavalrymen, were ordered to ride along the high ground south of the Auzon (*collibus . . . Haec procul ex oppido videbantur*). They left in company with some regular cavalry who were to make a demonstration over a wider area; but all were to converge on the same point by a long detour. These movements were observed from the town, for the hill of Gergovia afforded a bird's-eye view of our camp; but it was impossible for the enemy at that distance to be sure of what was impending.

One legion now started along the same route; after a short march it halted in the valley and lay hidden in some woods. The suspicion of the Gauls increased, and all their forces were rushed over to defend the Risolles-Gergovia ridge (*ad munitionem*). Directly I saw that the native camps had been evacuated the troops were ordered to veil their crests, hide their standards, and move in small groups, keeping well out of sight, from the camp towards Roche Blanche (*in minora* [*castra*]). The commanding officers of the various legions were carefully briefed and warned above all to keep their men in hand—not to let them advance too far through excessive zeal for battle or hope of loot. I reminded them that they would be at some disadvantage owing to their position on the hillside, a drawback which speed alone could overcome: the success of the operation depended on surprise, not on the force of their attack.

A straight line drawn from the town wall to the point where the ascent began measured nearly 2,000 yards: but the zigzag route covered by the troops in order to facilitate their climb naturally increased the distance. About half-way up the enemy had constructed a 6-foot wall which followed the horizontal contour of the ground and was intended to impede such an attack. The lower slopes were unoccupied, but the higher parts right up to the town wall were crowded with tribal encampments.

The signal was given to advance, and at the same moment the Aeduan contingent was ordered up the slope by another path on the right. The legions soon reached the outer wall, crossed it, and captured three camps. Their advance indeed had been so rapid that King Teutomatus of the Nitiobroges was surprised while taking an afternoon nap: when the troops broke into his tent, looking for plunder, he just managed to escape, stripped to the waist and riding a wounded horse.

As our first objective had now been achieved, a recall was sounded. The Tenth Legion, which I had with me, halted at once, but the others failed to hear the trumpet because of a wide depression that lay between us. The legionary commanders and junior officers followed my instructions and did all they could to restrain their men. The troops, however, fired with the hope of rapid success by the enemy's withdrawal, and by the memory of former victories, decided that no obstacle could withstand their courage, and continued the pursuit right up to the gates of Gergovia. The defenders stationed on the north wall were alarmed by the shouting that arose from every quarter of the town, and rushed out believing we had forced an entry. Women began throwing clothes and money from the ramparts, and leaned over with bared breasts and outstretched hands imploring our men to spare them and not to slaughter women and children as they had done at Bourges. Some of them were lowered by hand from the wall and gave themselves up. A centurion of the Seventh Legion, Lucius Fabius, with three soldiers of his company to help him, climbed on to the wall and pulled the others one by one after him: it later transpired that he had said in the hearing of his men on that very day that he expected rewards for the first up, as at Bourges, and that no one must attempt to forestall him.

Meanwhile the din was heard by the enemy detachment which had been sent to hold the Col des Goules (*munitionis causa*), and they soon received word by a succession of runners that the town was in our hands. Their mounted troops galloped ahead, followed by a huge swarm of infantry, and each man on arrival took up his position until a powerful force had gathered beneath the walls. The women, who a moment before had pleaded with the enemy, now began appealing to their own menfolk, leaning over in Gallic fashion with dishevelled hair and holding up their children for the men to see. It was a hopeless struggle: we occupied an inferior position and were also outnumbered; the charge uphill, too, and a prolonged engagement had exhausted the legions, who were no longer a match for troops newly come into action.

Seeing the enemy reinforced, and realizing the difficulty of fighting in these circumstances, I began to fear for the safety of my troops. I therefore sent an order to Titus Sextius who commanded at Roche Blanche (*minoribus castris*), telling him to bring out his force at once and station it at the foot of a hill opposite the Gallic right flank, so as to intercept the enemy's pursuit if he saw us driven from our position. I then moved the Tenth slightly forward and awaited developments.

There was fierce hand-to-hand fighting: the Gauls relied upon their position and superior numbers whilst our fellows trusted to their own courage. And now the Aedui appeared on our right: it will be remembered they were sent up by another route to create a diversion. The similarity of their armour to that of the enemy spread terror through the Roman ranks; for although they were seen to have their right shoulders uncovered—the usual badge of auxiliaries—the troops were convinced it was no more than a ruse of the enemy to deceive them.

At the same moment Fabius and his three companions on the wall were surrounded and killed; their bodies were thrown down from the rampart. Marcus Petronius, another centurion of the Seventh, was cut off by a crowd of natives while trying to break down one of the gates. Seriously wounded, and knowing he hadn't a dog's chance, he shouted to the men who followed him: 'I can't go with you: but it's my fault you're in this fix: too keen to make a show, that's me. I'll do what I can for you.' He then rushed among the enemy, killed two of them, and drove the rest back a short way from the gate. His comrades tried once more to save him; but again he cried: 'It's no good; I've lost

too much blood—I'm finished. Run for it while you can—
get back to the legion!' A moment later he fell fighting;
but he had saved his men.

Hard pressed on all sides the troops were forced from
their position with the loss of 46 centurions. The enemy
poured after them, but were checked by the Tenth which
was posted in reserve on a comparatively level stretch, and
this legion was covered in turn by battalions of the Thirteenth from Roche Blanche under Sextius, which had occupied some rising ground. As soon as each legion reached
the plain it halted, turned about, and faced the enemy:
Vercingetorix, however, withdrew his troops from the
lower slopes and retired behind his fortifications. We had
lost nearly 700 men.

Next day the legions paraded, and I reprimanded them
for their rashness and misplaced zeal in having decided their
own tactics, disobeyed the recall, and ignored the commands of their officers. Pointing out the danger of an
uphill engagement, I reminded them of the occasion at
Bourges when, although the enemy were caught without
their general or their cavalry, I had preferred to throw
away certain victory rather than suffer the smallest loss by
fighting uphill. While confessing my unbounded admira-
tion for the courage of men who refused to be daunted
by a fortified camp, a high mountain, and a walled town,
I condemned in no uncertain terms their indiscipline as
well as their presumption in thinking they knew more than
their commander-in-chief about the science of war and its
practical application. 'Men serving under me,' I concluded,
'are expected to show obedience and self-restraint no less
than valour in the field.' Before dismissing them, however,
I spoke a few words of encouragement, and told them not
to be disheartened by a reverse which was due more to the

ground over which they had been obliged to fight than to the enemy's military skill.

I had not changed my mind about the advisability of pulling out from Gergovia. The legions were formed up for battle in the plain; but as Vercingetorix would not come down, they returned to camp after a successful cavalry engagement. The repetition of this manœuvre next day was enough to damp the spirits of the Gauls and to restore confidence in our own troops. We therefore struck camp and started for Aeduan territory: the enemy still made no sign of following, and three days later we reached the Allier, rebuilt a bridge, and crossed.

Here I was greeted by Viridomarus and Eporedorix, who informed me that a great cavalry force under Litaviccus was on its way from Gergovia to rouse the Aedui, and they themselves must set off at once to secure the tribe's allegiance. There was already abundant evidence that the Aedui were disloyal, and it was probable that these two would precipitate revolt. But I decided not to detain them: the act might appear high-handed or suggest that I was afraid. Before they left I briefly recalled my services to their people, and compared the unhappy circumstances in which they had first appealed to me with their present condition: then they were shut up in their towns without lands or allies, forced to pay tribute, and to surrender hostages upon the most humiliating terms; now they were again a flourishing state, their power and prestige, indeed, surpassed any they had formerly enjoyed. With this reminder I let them go.

The Aeduan city of Nevers (*Noviodunum . . . Haeduorum*) is situated at a strategic point on the Loire. All Gallic hostages were detained there; it was the headquarters of our commissariat, the seat of our treasury, and a depot for the numerous remounts bought for use in this campaign

from Italy and the Peninsula. On reaching Nevers Eporedorix and Viridomarus learned that the great fortress of
Bibracte had opened its gates to Litaviccus: the Vergobret
Convictolitavis and many members of the council had em-
braced his cause, and envoys had been sent to negotiate a
formal alliance with Vercingetorix. They decided to make
the most of this advantage, massacred the garrison and Roman trading community, distributed the money and horses,
and arranged for the transfer of hostages to Bibracte. It
seemed impossible to defend Nevers, and, in order to render
the city useless as a Roman base, they burned it down.
Such grain as could be hurriedly loaded on to boats was
removed; the remainder was flooded or burned. They next
proceeded to mobilize troops in the neighbourhood, and
stationed detachments of varying strength along the Loire.
Their cavalry rode boldly through the district, hoping thereby to intimidate us or to cut us off from food supplies and
drive us back into the Province under stress of famine.
They were further encouraged by the swollen state of the
river: it was in flood as a result of melting snows, and appeared quite unfordable.

There was clearly no time to waste; if we had to build a
bridge, we might be attacked while doing so; and in that
case it would be better to fight a decisive action before the
enemy was reinforced. Some members of my staff advised
withdrawal to the Province: but this was out of the question. It would have been undignified and humiliating, apart
from the difficulty of crossing the Cévennes. Above all, I
was worried about Labienus and his four legions on the
Seine.

We reached the Loire in record time by a series of day
and night marches. Our mounted patrols discovered a ford
which proved useful in this emergency—at any rate the

men were able to carry their arms with head and shoulders above water. The cavalry formed a lane through the stream to break its force, and, as our unexpected arrival had upset the enemy's calculations, we got through without loss. Standing corn and herds of grazing cattle served to provision the army, which then resumed its march towards the Seine (*in Senones*).

Operations on the Seine

LABIENUS had received a new draft of recruits from Italy: he left it to guard the baggage at Sens, and moved with his four legions on Paris (*Luteciam*), which is situated on an island in the Seine. The Gauls heard of his approach: large tribal forces assembled, and the supreme command was entrusted to an Aulercan, Camulogenus, who was chosen, despite his great age, as their most experienced general. He learned that, in order to reach Paris, Labienus would have to cross the Essone (*perpetuam paludem*), a long stretch of marsh draining into the Seine. Here he took up his position and prepared to resist.

Labienus tried first, under cover of mantlets, to build a causeway of faggots overlaid with earth. Finding this too difficult, he stole out of camp between midnight and 1 a.m., retraced his steps, and halted at a point opposite Meclosedum, a Senonian fortress standing, like Paris, on an island in the river. There he seized about fifty boats, had them lashed hurriedly together to form a bridge, and threw his troops across. The remaining inhabitants were terrified by this surprise attack: many of them had been called up for military service, and Meclosedum fell without resistance. He then repaired a bridge which the Gauls had broken down some days earlier, and after crossing over to the right bank, began marching downstream towards Paris. Some refugees from Meclosedum reported this to the enemy, who ordered the burning of Paris and the destruction of all its bridges. Camulogenus now moved from the Essone (*a palude*) to the left bank of the Seine, and encamped before Paris opposite the Roman position.

By this time my retreat from Gergovia was common knowledge, and rumours were spreading of the Aeduan revolt and the success of a pan-Gallic rebellion. Some of the tribesmen in conversation with our native horse told them I had been checked at the Loire and obliged by famine to withdraw into the Province. The Bellovaci, moreover, had been restive for some time; when they heard of the Aeduan rising they began massing troops and making open preparations for war. The situation was fundamentally altered, and Labienus saw that he must revise his plans accordingly. He was no longer concerned with territorial gains or engaging the enemy: his one problem was how to get his troops back to Sens. He was threatened from the north by the Bellovaci, who had the reputation of being the finest soldiers in Gaul, and from the south by Camulogenus at the head of an army splendidly equipped and ready for immediate action. Finally, there was this great river which cut him off from his heavy equipment and reserves.

In these difficult and unforeseen circumstances, it was clear that everything depended on his own resolution. Towards evening, therefore, he summoned his officers, told them what he proposed to do, and asked them to carry out his instructions promptly and to the letter. Each of the boats which he had brought down from Meclosedum was placed in charge of a Roman knight with orders to move quietly soon after 10.30 p.m. to a point some four miles downstream, and to await him there. Five battalions, which he considered least reliable in action, were detached from a certain legion and detailed to guard the camp; the other five were ordered to leave just after midnight, taking all their equipment, and to march upstream with as much noise as possible. He also commandeered a number of small vessels which were to be rowed upstream with loud splashing of oars. Not long afterwards he stole out of camp with the three remaining legions, and made for the point where his flotilla lay at anchor. Enemy patrols stationed along the left bank heard nothing: at the height of a furious storm they were surprised and overpowered, after which the legions and their cavalry were quickly ferried across under supervision of the knights.

Just before daybreak the enemy received four simultaneous reports: there was an unusual commotion in the Roman camp; a long column was moving upstream; the sound of oars had been heard in the same direction; and troops were crossing lower down the river. This information convinced them that the Roman army was crossing at three separate points in preparation for a general withdrawal on account of the Aeduan revolt. Accordingly they also split up into three divisions, one of which was left to watch the Roman camp, while a small force was ordered upstream towards Meclosedum to overtake the boats, and the third went to meet Labienus.

By sunrise all the legions were across and within sight of the enemy. Labienus, in an order of the day, reminded his troops of their glorious traditions, of their brilliant successes in past years, and told them to imagine themselves fighting under the eye of their commander-in-chief who had so often led them to victory. In the initial stages of this action the enemy was held and thrown back by the Seventh

Legion on the right. On the left the Twelfth shattered his front ranks with a volley of pikes; but they continued to meet stiff resistance, the Gauls standing their ground to a man. Camulogenus was there in person, cheering on his men, and the result hung in the balance until the Seventh, whose company commanders learned of the situation on the right, appeared in the enemy's rear and charged. Even then not one of their opponents yielded an inch, but were all surrounded and killed. Camulogenus suffered the same fate.

The Gallic detachment on duty before the Roman camp heard that their main force was engaged, and moved up in support. They occupied the hill of Mont Parnasse (*collem*), but could not withstand the charge of our victorious troops, and were caught up in the general rout. All, except those who found cover among the woods and hills, were slaughtered by cavalry. Labienus returned to Sens, picked up his heavy equipment, and then rejoined me in full strength.

The Offensive Resumed

THE Aeduan revolt enlarged the theatre of war: their representatives journeyed through the various states, winning considerable support by bribery, influence, and prestige. The execution of some hostages whom I had left in their custody served to intimidate any who wavered. They asked Vercingetorix to visit them and concert plans, but he was met on arrival with a claim that the Aedui must hold supreme command. As no agreement could be reached on this point, a pan-Gallic council was summoned to meet at Bibracte, and was attended by delegates from almost every tribe. Among those not represented were the Remi and Lingones who adhered to a pro-Roman policy, while the Treveri remained neutral throughout because they lived too far away and were busy resisting German pressure. When the question was put to the vote, Vercingetorix was unanimously re-elected commander-in-chief.

The rejection of their claim was a bitter disappointment to the Aedui who considered it an affront to their dignity and regretted the loss of Roman patronage. But having once committed themselves to war, they dared not risk isolation, and it was with extreme reluctance that those promising young gentlemen, Eporedorix and Viridomarus, agreed to take orders from Vercingetorix.

Hostages and cavalry were required from every state, the former to be delivered at Gergovia within sixteen days. Fifteen thousand mounted troops were ordered to concentrate immediately at Bibracte; but having no intention of risking a pitched battle, Vercingetorix expressed himself satisfied if the infantry were brought up to its strength in previous campaigns: his cavalry was more than sufficient to prevent the Romans obtaining food supplies and forage, provided the civilian population co-operated by destroying their crops and burning their granaries, a sacrifice which would find its reward in the lasting autonomy of a Gallic empire. He then directed the Aedui and Segusiavi (a tribe living on the borders of our Province) to supply 10,000 infantry. Eight hundred cavalry were attached to this force, command of which was given to Eporedorix's brother with orders to invade Dauphiny and Savoy (*Allobroges*), where Vercingetorix imagined the Allobroges must still resent their subjugation by Rome nine years earlier. On this assumption he also dispatched secret agents as well as official deputations to enlist their support, promising the chieftains financial rewards, while dominion over the whole Roman Province was held out as a bait to their subjects. The Gabali and southernmost cantons of the Arverni were ordered to invade the Vivarais (*Helvios*), while the Ruteni and Cadurci ravaged Upper Languedoc (*fines Volcarum Arecomecorum*).

To deal with this emergency a force of twenty-two fresh battalions had been raised in the Transalpine Province by my deputy Lucius Caesar, and was stationed at various crucial points. The invasion of the Vivarais was opposed by the Helvii. They chose to engage the enemy in pitched battle, but were decisively beaten and forced to take refuge in their towns after suffering heavy casualties which included the loss of their chief magistrate, Caius Valerius Domnotaurus, son of Caburus. The Allobroges prepared a well-organized resistance by establishing a continuous line of defences on the Rhône.

I was aware that the enemy controlled a vastly superior force of cavalry: all roads were blocked, and it would have been impossible to obtain reinforcements from the Pro-

vince or from Italy. I therefore summoned German cavalry
with its attendant light infantry from beyond the Rhine,
where some tribes had submitted to us three years ago.
On arrival their horses proved unsuitable for the coming
operations, and they were supplied from our own stables
with remounts originally intended for our battalion commanders and other officers.

By this time the enemy had assembled an enormous force
consisting of an Arvernian division and the combined Gallic
cavalry. We were a few miles north of Dijon, heading for
Franche-Comté (*in Sequanos per extremos Lingonum fines iter
faceret*) to strengthen the provincial garrison, when Vercingetorix formed three camps about nine miles to the south-
west. He summoned a meeting of his cavalry commanders
and told them the hour of victory was at hand: the Romans were pulling out of Gaul and making for the Province. This withdrawal, he argued, might leave Gaul free
for the moment, but it would never guarantee lasting peace
and security, for they would only return in greater strength
and prolong the war indefinitely. He had therefore decided
to make a flank attack on the Roman transport column.
One of two things would then happen: either the legions
would halt and defend it, which would mean the end of
their march; or, more likely, they would abandon the
transport, run for their lives, and thereby lose essential
equipment together with their honour. As for the Roman
cavalry, he added, it was obvious that not a man would
dare to leave the column; but to inspire his own squadrons
with yet greater confidence, and to scare the enemy still
further, he proposed during the action to parade his infantry in battle formation outside their camps. These orders
were passed on to the men, and they clamoured for a
solemn oath forbidding any one who had not ridden at

least twice through the Roman lines access to his house and family. The proposal was adopted, and all were duly sworn.

Next day the Gallic cavalry was divided into three sections, two of which made a demonstration on either flank of our column while the third rode forward to block the road ahead of our vanguard. I split up my cavalry likewise into three divisions and ordered them to engage. Fighting broke out simultaneously along the whole length of the column, which halted and formed a hollow square with the transport inside. Wherever the cavalry appeared too hard pressed, troops in close order wheeled out to protect their flank, a manoeuvre which retarded the enemy's pursuit as well as strengthening our own men's morale. Eventually our German horse reached a hill-top away to the right, dislodged the enemy, and chased them with heavy casualties as far as the Suzon (*flumen*), where Vercingetorix was stationed with his infantry. The other Gallic squadrons witnessed this rout; they fled in order to avoid encirclement, and the slaughter became general. Three high-ranking Aeduans were taken prisoner and brought before me: they were Cotus, a cavalry commander and Convictolitavis's rival in the recent Vergobretal elections; Cavarillus, who had taken over Litaviccus's command after his desertion; and another man named Eporedorix, who had led his people in their struggle with the Sequani before I came to Gaul.

Alesia

AFTER the defeat of his cavalry Vercingetorix withdrew the infantry from their positions described above; he gave orders for the transport to follow him with all possible speed, and began retreating upon the Mandubian stronghold of Alesia. I detailed two legions to guard our heavy equipment, which had been removed to higher ground, and pursued him until nightfall. Some 3,000 of his rearguard had been killed by the time we encamped next day below the fortress. The Gauls were seriously concerned over the rout of their horse, for it was upon that arm they principally relied: so, after reconnoitring the position of the town, I called on the troops in an order of the day for their wholehearted effort, and began the investment of Alesia.

The fortress itself stood on the summit of a hill, and was clearly impregnable except by blockade. Washed on the north and south by the Oze and Ozerain (*duo duabus ex partibus flumina*), it was closely surrounded on three sides by a range of heights, the mean altitude of which equalled that of Alesia itself; while the plain of Les Laumes (*planities*) extended for about three miles to the west. The Gallic army covered the whole eastern slope below the ramparts, and had fortified their camp with a ditch and 6-foot wall. The Roman lines now in course of construction had a perimeter of just over nine and a half miles: eight camps lay at strategic points along this circuit and were linked together by twenty-three redoubts which were guarded against surprise attack in the daytime by pickets and at night by strong standing patrols.

While the work was in progress a bitterly contested cavalry engagement was fought in the plain. Our men found themselves in difficulties; but the German horse went to their assistance and the legions were drawn up outside their respective camps. This last measure gave our squadron fresh confidence: the enemy were thrown back in disorder, and their very numbers made escape impossible. Hotly pursued by the Germans, and unable to crowd through the narrow gateways, some of them dismounted and tried to cross the ditch or climb the wall. Their casualties were heavy.

The legions were then ordered to make a short advance as if closing in, and the Gauls behind their own defences were as terrified as the rest: believing a general assault imminent they gave the alarm; but some of them broke and fled into the citadel, where Vercingetorix had the gates shut for fear his camp should be abandoned. The Germans killed many of the fugitives and took a number of horses before retiring.

Vercingetorix now decided to evacuate the remainder of his cavalry by night before the Roman lines were completed. His parting instructions were that all should get back to their respective tribes and impress for service every one of military age. He reminded them of all they owed him, emphasized the fact that his fate was entirely in their hands, and implored them not to repay his endeavours in the cause of liberation by betraying him to a merciless enemy. Any indifference on their part, he said, would involve not only his own destruction, but that also of 80,000 first-class troops into the bargain. He had calculated that existing supplies of grain would last on short rations for a month, and might even hold out longer on the basis of yet more drastic economy.

The cavalry, therefore, made their way out in silence through a gap in our lines. Units stationed outside the town were then recalled, and Vercingetorix gave orders on pain of death that all stocks of corn must be deposited at his headquarters: it was doled out in small quantities at a time, but the large herds of cattle, which had been rounded up by the Mandubii, were distributed individually and at once.

Vercingetorix believed these preparations would enable him to fight on until he was relieved; but his plans were made known to us by deserters and prisoners of war. Accordingly we undertook the construction of more extensive earthworks. At the foot of the western slope a 20-foot trench was dug with perpendicular sides, and new lines of contravallation were begun about 650 yards further west: it was impossible to man the whole of that vast perimeter, but it was none the less essential to protect the works against a sudden night attack and to keep the workers themselves beyond range of enemy missiles in the daytime. Two trenches of equal depth and 14½ feet wide were dug. The inner one ran across perfectly level ground and was filled with water diverted from the Ozerain and its affluent, the Rabutin (*ex flumine*). Behind these trenches was a 12-foot rampart and palisade strengthened with an embattled breastwork, from the foot of which there projected a row of forked branches to check the enemy's ascent. Towers were erected at intervals of about 130 yards along the entire circuit of fortifications.

During the construction of these immense siege-works it was still necessary to send out men to collect materials and grain. As these parties had to travel some distance, our forces were greatly reduced, and as the Gauls were making periodical attacks in the form of mass sorties from several gates at once I decided to elaborate the defences. Tree-trunks or very stout branches were cut down, stripped of their bark, sharpened at the top, and fixed immovably in long trenches 5 feet deep. They were in rows of five, interlaced, so that any one trying to get through them would inevitably be impaled on the points. The soldiers called them 'tombstones'. In front of them again, and arranged in diagonal rows to form a series of quincunxes, we dug pits 3 feet deep, tapering gradually towards the bottom. In these were embedded smooth logs as thick as a man's thigh, sharpened at the top, fire-hardened, and set to protrude no more than about 3 inches from the ground.

To make them more secure, earth was thrown into the pits and trodden down hard to a depth of one foot, the hole being then concealed with twigs and brushwood. These traps were planted in groups of eight rows three feet apart, and the men nicknamed them 'lilies' because of their resemblance to that flower. In front of them was a densely strewn area of logs nearly a foot long, sunk right into the ground but sprouting iron hooks, and referred to by the troops as 'goads'.

When these defences were complete we built a thirteen-mile line of circumvallation: it followed roughly the same plan as the foregoing, and was parallel with it so far as the ground permitted, but faced in the opposite direction to meet an attack from the west. Its purpose was to secure the garrisons on the contravallation from encirclement, irrespective of the size of the attacking force. In order to avoid the danger of our fellows having to leave camp when the relieving army was near, every man was ordered to provide himself with a month's supply of corn and fodder.

During these operations before Alesia a council of Gallic chieftains overruled Vercingetorix's proposal to call up every one of military age. It was feared that in so vast an army, representing so many tribes, discipline would collapse, the several units would tend to coalesce, and the commissariat would become disorganized. It was therefore decided to require a specified number of troops from the various states as follows:

1. Aedui (including their dependants:
   Segusiavi, Ambivareti, Brannovices)   35,000
2. Arverni (with their dependants: Eleuteti, Cadurci,
   Gabali, Vellavii)   35,000
3. Sequani, Senones, Bituriges, Santoni, Ruteni, Carnutes   *each* 12,000

4. Bellovaci, Lemovices	*each*	10,000
5. Pictones, Turoni, Parisii, Helvetii	*each*	8,000
6. Andes, Ambiani, Mediomatrici, Petrocorii, Nervii, Morini, Nitiobroges	*each*	6,000
7. Aulerci, Cenomani, Atrebates	*each*	5,000
8. Veliocasses		4,000
9. Esuvii and Aulerci Eburovices		3,000
10. Rauraci and Boii		2,000
11. The Armorican tribes (Coriosolites, Redones, Ambibarri, Caletes, Osismi, Veneti, Lexovii, Venelli) on the north-west seaboard		30,000
		290,000

Note. The Bellovaci did not send their full quota: they announced their intention of running a private war of their own without outside interference. However, at the request of Commius, who had some personal claim to their respect, they did provide a couple of thousand men.

I have already mentioned the loyal and useful service rendered by Commius in Britain three years earlier. In return I had declared his tribe autonomous and exempt from taxation, and had appointed him overlord of the Morini. But the Gallic states were unanimous in their resolve to win back freedom and re-establish their military reputation. They devoted themselves wholeheartedly to the prosecution of war, nor would Commius himself be influenced by present favours or the memory of our earlier friendship. Assisted by an advisory committee of the states he received joint command of the relief force with the two Aeduans, Viridomarus and Eporedorix, and Vercassivellaunus, a son-in-law of Vercingetorix. This force, which was concentrated in Burgundy (*in Haeduorum finibus*), consisted of 8,000 cavalry and some 250,000 foot, which started for Alesia after a call-over and review. The Gauls were full of en-

219

thusiasm, and confident that the mere sight of so vast an
armament would paralyse the enemy, who would have
to fight on two fronts as the besieged were due to launch
an attack simultaneously with the appearance of the relieving army.

The garrison of Alesia was ignorant of these preparations:
the day on which they had expected to be relieved was now
past, and their food supplies were exhausted. An assembly
was called to discuss the situation, and various opinions
were put forward. Some were for capitulation, others for
trying to break out now, while their strength lasted. The
speech of Critognatus, however, deserves to be recorded
for its monstrous and inhuman cruelty. He was a noble
Arvernian whose word carried very considerable weight:

I shall not [he said] comment on the view of those who advocate
the degradation of slavery under the euphemism of capitulation:
they should not be regarded as citizens or admitted to this assembly.
I am concerned rather with those who suggest a break-out. Your
approval of such a course argues at least some vestige of our
traditional valour; but surely the inability to endure privation for
a little while is evidence of weakness, not of courage. Men ready
to embrace death are never far to seek; the rare bird is he who
will suffer hardship patiently. However, I entertain the greatest
respect for those of you who want to fight your way out; and
I might approve the plan if I foresaw it would involve nothing
worse than the loss of our own lives. But in coming to a decision
we must consider Gaul as a whole, all those whom we have summoned to our aid. How do you suppose our relatives and kinsmen
will feel if they have to fight so to speak over the corpses of 80,000
dead? I ask you not to deprive them of your support when they
are ready to risk everything for your sake. Do not, by your folly,
your rashness, or your cowardice ruin our country and subject
her to everlasting slavery. Have you doubts as to their loyalty
and determination because they were not here at the appointed
time? Do you imagine the Romans are working day after day on

their new lines simply for their own amusement? True the exist-
ence of these lines prevents your receiving messages of reassurance
from without: but look! the Romans are making frantic efforts
day and night; they are your witnesses that relief is on its way.
What, then, is my advice? I think we should do what our fathers
did in their struggle with the Cimbri and Teutones—a much less
critical episode than this. Shut up in their towns and, like ourselves, confronted with starvation, they would not give in: they
fed on the flesh of those who were too young or too old to fight.
Even if there were no precedent for such a deed, I would still
urge you to establish one now and hand it on to your posterity. I
say there is no comparison between the earlier war and this: the
Cimbri devastated Gaul and did her untold harm, but they eventually retired and sought fresh fields, leaving us in possession of our
lands, free to enjoy our rights and to live under our own laws.
It is not so with Rome. Rome has but one purpose: envy is her
spur; she knows the ancient glory of our race, she has learned
our might in war, and therefore she means to occupy our native
land and bind upon us the yoke of servitude for ever. That has
always been the policy of Rome. Maybe you have no experience
of conditions abroad; but look nearer home, look at your own
Gaul, turned into a Roman province with new laws and institutions, prostrate beneath the heel of Rome.

The debate concluded with a decision to expel from the
town all those whose age or infirmity rendered them unable
to bear arms. It was also resolved to try every expedient
before adopting Critognatus's shameful proposition, which
might, however, be forced upon them if relief were delayed
much longer and the alternative were unconditional surrender. The Mandubii, who had received them into Alesia,
were driven out with their wives and children. They came
over to our lines and made a piteous appeal to be received
and fed, if only as slaves: but guards were posted on the
rampart with orders to refuse them admission.

The relieving force under Commius and his fellow commanders arrived before Alesia and encamped on the heights of Mussy-la-Fosse (*in colle*) about a mile to the west of our circumvallation. Next day their cavalry came out and occupied the whole plain of Les Laumes (*planitiem*) while their infantry took up a position on some high ground slightly farther back. Their presence was observed from Alesia, which had a bird's-eye view of the plain, and the besieged crowded together, giving vent to their joy, and congratulating one another on their impending deliverance. They then emerged in full strength and halted under the town walls while some of them came down and filled up our 20-foot ditch preparatory to risking an attack.

I therefore disposed the whole of my infantry along the two lines of fortification, in such a way that every man would in future know his exact position. The cavalry was ordered to engage, and as our camps on the surrounding heights commanded a full view of the field, the whole army looked on intently to witness the result. The Gauls had posted archers and light infantry among their mounted troops in order to give them cover if they had to fall back, and to strengthen their resistance to our charge. Some of our fellows, surprised and wounded by these troops, were obliged to retire. The enemy, sure that their cavalry had the upper hand (for we were clearly outnumbered), began cheering and shouting encouragement from Alesia and Mussy-la-Fosse (*ex omnibus partibus et ii qui in munitionibus continebantur et ii qui ad auxilium convenerant*). As the action took place in full view of everybody, and no act of bravery or cowardice could pass unnoticed, the thirst for glory and the fear of disgrace were alike powerful incentives on both sides. Fighting had lasted from about midday to sunset when our German cavalry charged in mass formation: the enemy were hurled back, and as their mounted divisions fled, the archers were cut off and slaughtered. The rest of our horse galloped up from other parts of the field, and chased the fleeing squadrons right up to their camp, giving them no chance to rally. Vercingetorix's men re-entered the town, bitterly disappointed and almost in despair.

After an interval of one day, during which they prepared vast quantities of faggots, scaling-ladders, and grappling hooks, the relief force stole out of camp at midnight and advanced towards the circumvallation. Suddenly raising a cheer to warn the besieged of their approach, they began throwing faggots into the trenches, tried to drive us from the rampart with a hail of arrows and stones hurled from slings or by hand, and, indeed, used every known method of assault. Vercingetorix heard their shout: he sounded the alarm, and paraded his men outside the walls while the legions moved to their appointed stations and beat off the attack with one-pounder slings and stakes piled at intervals along the rampart. Our artillery meanwhile kept up a steady fire; but it was too dark to see, and there were heavy casualties on both sides. Mark Antony and Trebonius, however, who had been entrusted with the defence of that sector, brought up men from the redoubts in rear of the fighting line and reinforced such points as they saw particularly hard pressed.

As long as the Gauls kept well clear of the defences they gained some advantage from superior fire-power; but as they came nearer they were caught on the 'goads', or sank into the pits and were impaled on the 'lilies', while others were killed by heavy siege spears discharged from the towers. Their losses were everywhere enormous, but at daybreak they had failed to penetrate our defences. Afraid, therefore, of being taken on their right flank by an attack from the camps on Réa and Flavigny (*ex superioribus castris*), they fell back on their own lines. Meanwhile the besieged had lost a good deal of time bringing out their assault apparatus and filling up the first line of 'tombstone' trenches. Before they reached the main fortifications they learned that the relieving force had again withdrawn, and so returned once more to Alesia having accomplished exactly nothing.

After this second disastrous repulse, the Gauls held a council of war, and, by calling in men familiar with the neighbourhood, they learned the positions and strength of our camps on the surrounding heights. It had been impossible to entrench Mont Réa (*colles*), on the north, because of its huge circumference, and we had been obliged to establish a camp there at the foot of a gentle slope which would give an assailant some small advantage. It was occupied by two legions commanded respectively by Gaius Antistius Reginus and Gaius Caninius Rebilus. Following patrol reconnaissance of the locality the enemy commanders, having agreed in secret on their objective and plan of action, detailed 60,000 men from the most warlike tribes to launch an attack at noon under Vercassivellaunus. Leaving camp an hour or so after sunset, he completed his march just before daybreak and ordered his troops to rest under cover of Mont Réa (*post montem*). As zero hour approached, he began moving on the Roman camp while the Gallic cavalry advanced towards our circumvallation and infantry paraded in strength outside their encampment.

Vercingetorix saw these movements from the citadel of Alesia: he had faggots, poles, mantlets, grappling-hooks, and other apparatus brought out in readiness for an assault on our fortifications. There was fighting along the whole line, and the Gauls made desperate efforts to overwhelm the weaker points in the defence. My troops found difficulty in meeting these simultaneous attacks. They were unnerved, too, by the shouting in their rear, which impressed them with a sense of their utter dependence on the courage of others; for it is generally the invisible that is most alarming.

Standing on the north-west slope of Flavigny (*idoneum locum nactus*), I could see the whole battle-field, and was thus able to send up reinforcements wherever they were needed. Both sides realized that the crisis demanded a supreme effort: the Gauls knew that everything depended on their smashing through our fortifications, while the legions foresaw an end of all their labours if they could only hold

their ground. The fighting was most bitter at Mont Réa (*ad superiores munitiones*), where the enemy's downhill thrust told heavily against us: some of them flung javelins while others advanced under locked shields, the entire force being constantly relieved by fresh waves of men. Earth was heaped against the fortifications at all points, enabling them to climb the rampart and at the same time covering the traps which we had laid. I received word that the men were tiring and short of ammunition. Six battalions were therefore sent to their relief under Labienus, who had orders to stand his ground unless and until the position became absolutely untenable, in which case he was to regroup and fight his way out. I then visited other parts of the field to encourage the exhausted troops with a reminder that to give way now would undo all their former victories.

Vercingetorix had realized by this time the hopelessness of trying to break through our defences in the plain: he now decided to storm the contravallation where it crossed the heights of Flavigny (*loca praerupta*), and accordingly moved his assault apparatus over to that sector. The defenders were forced from their towers under a hail of missiles, the trenches filled in with faggots and earth, the rampart and breastworks torn down with grappling-hooks. Several battalions led by young Brutus were ordered to reinforce the position, then more under Gaius Fabius. Finally, as the struggle grew more desperate, I myself took up a fresh detachment: the balance was restored and the enemy fell back.

I then started for Mont Réa (*eo quo Labienum miserat*), taking five battalions from the nearest redoubt. One detachment of cavalry was ordered to accompany us while another rode round the circumvallation to take the enemy's rear. The trenches and rampart had failed against the Gallic assault; fortunately, however, Labienus had been able to concentrate eleven battalions from the redoubts in his sector, and he now sent to warn me of his next move. I hurried forward to be present at this engagement.

The enemy recognized my scarlet cloak, and then saw my combined force moving down the slopes, which were clearly visible from Mont Réa (*de superioribus locis*). As they

226

joined battle both sides raised a cheer which was taken up by the soldiers on the rampart and along the whole line of fortifications. The legionaries dispensed with pikes, and had got to work with their swords when the Gauls suddenly beheld our mounted squadrons in their rear as fresh battalions of infantry closed in from the south. They broke and fled, but were intercepted by the cavalry and mown down. Sedulius, chief magistrate and commander of the Lemovices was killed; Vercassivellaunus was taken prisoner in the rout; and I was presented with seventy-four Gallic standards. Very few of that great army got back safely to camp.

Vercingetorix witnessed the rout and slaughter of his countrymen: he gave up all hope, and withdrew once again into Alesia, while the camp on Mussy-la-Fosse was hurriedly abandoned (*ex castris Gallorum fuga*). Had not our men been tired out after a long day's work, in the line or in reserve, the entire enemy force might well have been annihilated. As it was, the cavalry went out just after midnight and overtook their rearguard, many of whom were cut down or taken prisoner. The survivors made for home.

On the following day Vercingetorix addressed a meeting of the chiefs, and explained that he had embarked upon this war not for private ends, but in his country's cause. 'Now,' he said, 'I must bow to the decrees of Fate.' He then invited the assembly to palliate the wrath of Rome in whatever way they chose, either by putting him to death or by delivering him up alive. A deputation having referred the matter to me, they were ordered to surrender their weapons together with their leading men. Seated, therefore, on the rampart of our camp, I received the capitulation of Alesia: their chieftains were marched out, Vercingetorix was handed over, and all their arms were stacked. The Aeduan and Arvernian prisoners were spared as likely to prove useful in regaining the allegiance of those tribes; the rest were distributed as loot among the whole army, one to every man.

After the fall of Alesia I travelled to Burgundy (*in Haeduos*), where the Aedui made their submission. An Arvernian delegation also arrived with promises of the tribe's obedience to any orders I might give: they were instructed to deliver numerous hostages. Having repatriated some 20,000 Aeduan and Arvernian prisoners I sent the legions into winter quarters as follows. Two legions and some cavalry under Labienus, with Marcus Sempronius Rutilus as second in command, were stationed in Franche-Comté (*in Sequanos*). Gaius Fabius and Lucius Minucius Basilus took their respective legions to Champagne (*in Remis*) with orders to protect the Remi against the neighbouring Bellovaci. Titus Sextius, Caninius, and Reginus, with one legion each, proceeded respectively to Berry (*in Bituriges*), Le Rauergne (*in Rutenos*), and the territory of the Ambivareti. Cicero and Publius Sulpicius Rufus were ordered to Chalon-sur-Saône (*Cavilloni*) and Mâcon (*Matisconi*) in Burgundy (*in Haeduis*) to supervise the corn supply, while I myself decided to winter at Bibracte. On receipt of my dispatches for this year a public thanksgiving of twenty days was celebrated at Rome.